THE ART OF BEING BRILLIANT

SECOND EDITION

DR ANDY COPE & ANDY WHITTAKER

brought to life by Amy Bradley

CAPSTONE
A Wiley Brand

Registered Office(s)
John Wiley & Sons, Inc., 111 River Street, Hoboken, NJ 07030, USA
John Wiley & Sons Ltd, The Atrium, Southern Gate, Chichester, West Sussex, PO19 8SQ, UK

For details of our global editorial offices, customer services, and more information about Wiley products visit us at www.wiley.com.

Wiley also publishes its books in a variety of electronic formats and by print-on-demand. Some content that appears in standard print versions of this book may not be available in other formats.

Library of Congress Cataloging-in-Publication Data Is Available:

ISBN 9780857089861 (Paperback)
ISBN 9780857089885 (ePDF)
ISBN 9780857089878 (ePub)

Cover Design: Amy Bradley

Set in 11/16.5 pt Roboto-Regular by Straive, Chennai, India.

SKY10070408_032224

To the crazy bunch:

Martin, Daz, Lou, Izzie, Pouli, Sanj, Jase, Mikey, Nikki, Suze, Taz, Flis, Jen, M, Kev, JP, Wolfie, Nige, Wee P, Indy, Errol, H, Sof, Will, Ollie, Chewy, Peter ...

Awe, admiration and big THANKS.

xxx

A quick note: Some content is shared with our sister book, The Art of Being a BRILLIANT Teenager. That's because the messages about positivity, resilience, kindness, confidence, strengths, goals, purpose and relationships are universal. To 'be your best self' and 'live your best life' you need to adopt a consistent set of principles, whether you're age 14 or 44, or 114.

Running order

ONE: Jimmy's Diary

PAGE: 01

TWO: Fishing for life

PAGE: 05

THREE: Shiny HAPPY people

PAGE: 19

FOUR: The curse of mediocrity

PAGE: 35

FIVE: Can God do a handstand?

PAGE: 51

A true story about a toaster

SIX: You're toast.
PAGE: 63

BONUS OFFERING: The 3Rs
PAGE: 73

Relationships, relationships, relationships!!

SEVEN: Master Mind.
An instruction manual for your brain
PAGE: 85

EIGHT: Kindness is a super-power
PAGE: 101

NINE: Your F*ckit List
PAGE: 119

TEN: The 90/10 Principle
PAGE: 137

Must have more!!

"Everything Speaks"

ELEVEN:
The upside down
PAGE: 151

TWELVE:
Fearing the wurst
PAGE: 165

THIRTEEN:
No hard feelings
PAGE: 173

FOURTEEN:
≋HUGE≋
goals and
BIG
strengths
PAGE: 189

FIFTEEN:
Omnipotent handstands
PAGE: 205

About the writing team PAGE: 221

Epilogue: Life by PowerPoint. Clive's story PAGE: 226

Enjoy yourself, it's later than you think.
A hit for The Specials, 1980

Your pre-read check list.

Before the off, please ensure you have:

- ✓ Your mind switched to open.
- ✓ Your 'offence button' deactivated.
- ✓ Learning mode, fully engaged.
- ✓ Angry mode, off.
- ✓ Willingness to take action, set to 'very'.
- ✓ Your sense of humour, turned up to the max.
- ✓ Your likelihood to leave a 5-star Amazon review set to 'deffo'.
- ✓ A cup of tea/coffee/7-Up.
- ✓ A Werther's Original or mint humbug.

↑ flick it on!

Thank you.

ONE: Jimmy's Diary

Andy c

Andy w

Amy

The warmest of welcomes from Amy, Andy W and myself. I'll do most of the talking, Amy will do the pics and Andy W will steal the show.

We weren't sure where or how to start, so we've plumped for Jimmy's Diary. On face value it's poignant and wonderful and then, all of a sudden, you can't breathe.

Be warned, Jimmy's Diary has a mic-drop moment ...

He hadn't been up there for years. In the faint light of the attic, the old man shuffled across to a pile of boxes that lay near one of the cobwebbed windows. Brushing aside the dust, he began to lift out some old photo albums.

His search began with the fond recollection of the love of his life. She was long gone but he knew that somewhere in these albums was the photo he was looking for. It was the black-and-white one, when she had that smile.

Setting aside one of the dusty albums, he pulled from the box what appeared to be a diary from his son's childhood. Opening the yellowed pages, he glanced over the entries and his lips turned up at the corners in an unconscious smile. His eyes shone and he chuckled aloud. He realised he wasn't just reading the words ... he could hear them, spoken by his young son who'd grown up far too fast in this very house. In the utter silence of the attic, the earnest words of a six-year-old worked their magic and the old man was carried back to a time almost forgotten.

The spidery handwriting reflected on important issues for a six year-old – school, football, holidays, arguments with his big sister – entry after entry stirred a sentimental hunger in the old man's heart. But it was accompanied by a painful memory that his son's simple recollections of those days didn't tally with his own. The old man's wrinkles became more deeply etched.

He remembered that he'd kept a business diary from around the same time. He closed his son's journal and turned to leave, having forgotten the cherished photo that had triggered his initial search. Hunched over to stop himself from bumping his head on the beams, the old man stepped down the wooden stairway to his office.

He opened a glass cabinet door, reached in and sought his business diary. He placed the journals side by side. His was leather bound, his name embossed in gold. His son's was tatty and frayed with a hand-drawn picture on the front. The old man ran a bony finger across the name 'Jimmy' scribbled on the cover.

He turned the pages of his business journal and read some of the entries. There were notes from meetings, often very detailed. Every single day was crammed with business appointments. Sometimes the evenings too. He remembered back to those times … he sure was driven in his career. It was for the love of his family that he'd chased success so hard. The old man was drawn to an entry much shorter than the rest. In his own neat handwriting were these words, 'Wasted a whole day fishing with Jimmy. Didn't catch a thing!'

With a deep sigh and a shaking hand, he took Jimmy's journal and found the boy's entry for the same day, 4th June. Large scrawling letters pressed deep into the paper read …

'Went fishing with my dad. Best day of my life.'

[Mic drop]

#ArtOfBrillBook #JimmysDiary

Many men go fishing all of their lives without knowing it's NOT fish they're after

Henry David Thoreau

philosopher, poet and political activist

4

TWO: Fishing for life

In which we recover from Jimmy's Diary by suggesting that the search is over. You know all those annoying gurus who say that you should 'look within', well guess what, *they're right!*

This chapter leaves you on the ropes, punch drunk, before rescuing you with a cool question, a game of *Real or Fake*, and some small print.

Oh, and while you're at it, look out for the number 4000. It's important.

WAKEY-WAKEY!

The modern world is full of contradictions, fake news and half-truths. It's given us the rallying cry of YOLO, as though the realisation that You Only Live Once is enough to galvanise you into action. This well-meaning mantra is the opposite of the truth. In actual fact, YODO is how life really works.

You Only *Die* Once, you get to live every single day.

The question is, how? How am I supposed to live my best life and be my best self, when the world is sometimes hell bent on knocking me sideways?

This is where *The Art of Being Brilliant* works its magic. It's the shrillest of alarms , a rude awakening that encourages you to rub the sleep from your eyes and see life differently. *Wakey-wakey!* You've slept in but it's not too late. It's never too late! Our job is to tap you on the shoulder and be with you as you wake up to the magnificence of life.

Andy W and I have been working for numerous years delivering keynotes and workshops in businesses and schools. A few years ago we developed a workshop that we boldly called 'The Art of Being Brilliant'. And do you know what, it's really rather amazing!

It's amazingness comes from subterfuge. Whisper this bit quietly … we deliver it in workplaces but it isn't really about work! You're reading the book version of the workshop, which is more closely aligned to Jimmy's Diary than whatever your nine-to-five is.

ALL aboard the...

It has become very clear to us over the past couple of decades that the people we work with already know everything there is to know about creating a happy and successful life. Everyone has all the resources they need – I mean, how exciting is that! You already have all the answers! It's just that society has developed a bad case of collective amnesia. The majority of people have totally blanked their wisdom, and the result is that we hit peaks of happiness and positivity on an ad hoc basis. We feel 'brilliant' sporadically, sometimes quite by accident. We wait for the right conditions, or a special occasion, without realising that life is the ultimate special occasion.

♥ **Focusing fact**
The average human heart will beat 2.5 billion times. That equates to approximately 28,000 days, or 4000 weeks.

The problem is that most people are looking for their personal best in the wrong place. Richard Wilkins[1] describes it brilliantly when he talks of people searching for happiness, fulfilment and

1. Check our Richard's amazing work at www.theministryofinspiration.com

positive feelings in the filing cabinet marked 'external'. They're super-busy looking for happiness 'out there' somewhere.

He's in line with all those annoying gurus who suggest you look for happiness within. Bad news, we agree with those annoying gurus! We believe that most people are looking for happiness and fulfilment in the wrong filing cabinet. We think you should start looking for happiness and fulfilment in the filing cabinet marked 'internal'.

Happiness is not an experience, it's an *in-sperience*. All the great feelings you ever felt are already inside you!

So chill, the search is over!

Our job has become easy. We don't have to teach anything. All we have to do is devise a cunning way of reconnecting people with their own internal resources, putting them in touch with information that has been buried in their unconscious mind. Or, to keep it simple, get them to look in the right filing cabinet ... the one marked 'internal'.

Oh, and this book is the key!

It's designed to make you think, and maybe even chuckle, but the underlying message is deadly serious. We're talking about you and your life. Excuse the bluntness of these next few words, but nobody gets out alive. Ultimately, when your death rattle comes, it's not dying you're really afraid of – it's getting to the end of life without having really lived it! So don't just read *The Art of Being Brilliant, be it!* The results will reverberate positively at work and home. It's become abundantly clear to us that 'success' isn't about becoming a different person. It's a matter of finding out what really works for you, *and doing more of it!*

Punch drunk

Life can feel a bit like Mario Kart. It's fast, furious and unforgiving. There are banana skins aplenty!

'The future's so bright, I gotta wear shades.'

1986 hit for Timbuk 3.

But mental health is no game.

This is the age of anxiety. Depression is rife. Panic attacks and a gazillion other mental health issues are on the rise. Our wonderful NHS is fighting tooth and nail to patch us up and get us out of the door.

You'll have noticed that *The Art of Being Brilliant* is a very bold, in-your-face title. I guess we could have called it *The Art of Being Bang Average,* or *A User's Guide to Living a Bog-Standard Life* but, quite frankly, what's the point? In a world where there's a lot of talk about *living your best life* and *being your best self, The Art of Being Brilliant* is the art and science of exactly that.

Yes, science! This book is evidence based. That means it's got some academic oomph behind it. If you want my unexpurgated PhD thesis in all its sesquipedalian vainglorious verbosity you can download the scholarly behemoth from here: https://www. artofbrilliance.co.uk/Dr-Andy-Cope-Thesis.pdf

Go wrestle with it to your heart's content.

This is the opposite of that!

Hippopotomonstrosesquippedaliophobia: the fear of long words.

I've been super-careful to remove all the lumpy words and replace them with common sense, do-able principles and fabulous fun. Andy and I have deliberately chosen to give the book a light touch, but I promise you it's not lightweight. The aim is to challenge you – and I mean really challenge you – to re-think your thinking and turn your gaze away from the meaningless towards the meaningful.

This is more important than ever because the world has morphed from fast and furious into a full-on contact sport. The 3Cs of challenge, change and complexity are punching hard. As a result, there are lots of people on the ropes, teetering on the brink of exhaustion, anxiety or total knock-out.

In the previous millennium, we used to call it stress. Now it's burnout or 'mental pneumonia'. Life does its best to leave you lots of clues, hidden in plain sight.

Ignore them at your peril …

If the people you love are starting to irritate you, or if your work colleagues are driving you mad – CLUE – it's not about them!

Agresso:

lack of coffee

Brenda was delighted to have discovered what STRESSED was when spelt backwards

If you haven't got time to do what you know is good and healthy (you mindlessly devour a meal deal while sitting at your laptop, skip your daily walk, can't make the gym, haven't got time to cook from scratch, stay up late to finish your emails, haven't got time to pop in and see your mum) – CLUE – burnout is nipping at your heels.

But, of course, you're stoic and tough so you stagger on regardless. Punch drunk by life, it's easy to let your brilliance slip. Rather than rising to the challenges it's more likely you'll be wanting a signed apology from the world for the way it's been treating you.

The harsh reality is that the world doesn't care how you feel. If your plan is to sit patiently and wait for an apology, you'll die waiting. It's the same with relationships and success.

'Sitting patiently' is passive.

Talk is cheap, and grumbling is free. *Gratis. Compliments of the house.* Complaining is an all-you-can-eat buffet. Sure, it'll give you acid in your stomach, but you can consume as much low-level bellyaching as you want.

The Art of Being Brilliant is your literary chamomile tea. Designed to ease the burning, it's written to help you thrive – yes, *thrive* – not survive, or get by, or muddle through.

Real or fake?

When I was a kid my teacher pulled me to one side and asked, 'Andy, what do you want to be when you grow up?'

I'm nine years old and I've got literally no idea. 'I dunno, Sir,' my head buzzing with nothingness. Then an idea popped into my skull, 'Tell you what, Sir, when I grow up I'm gonna be an astronaut.'

I beamed up at him hopefully and he smiled back, pitifully. 'You're from Derby,' he said, 'so do you want to have another go?'

Undeterred by his clumsy words, I beamed up at my teacher and said, 'Okay then, if I can't be an astronaut, how about a window cleaner?'

'Excellent,' he purred. 'You should aim for that.'

That exchange isn't about how a deflating comment can ruin a child's life. It made no impact on me whatsoever. I'm re-telling it because 'What do you want to be when you grow up?' up is a lame question to ask a nine-year-old.

I prefer a tweaked version of the same question, which is a thousand times more powerful and just happens to be the bedrock of this book:

What kind of person do you want to be when you grow up?
Because, do you know what, I could answer that at age 9, and 15,

and 37 and 56, and I still will at age 95 and three-quarters. For me, it's deadly simple: *I want to be the best me I can be.*

I'm guessing your answer will be exactly the same. You want to be a nice, kind, loving, positive, optimistic, honest, good, grateful, confident, friendly, happy, successful human being. Which of course you absolutely are, *sometimes*. But with the world punching so hard, we can sometimes have our best intentions knocked out of us.

But there's one more word that is super-important. I'll get to it via a little story I wrote called 'Real or Fake'. Here's a snippet:

Jake was in wondering mode. He was trying to work out what he preferred so he wrote a list called real or fake, and it went something like this – Orange flavour, or an actual orange?
Freshly ground coffee, or instant?
Mr Whippy, or Ben & Jerry's?
A postcard, or the actual holiday?
Fake lashes, or real?
Coca-Cola, or supermarket own brand cola?
Raw or photoshopped selfie?
Blackpool Tower, or the Eiffel Tower?
A real flesh-and-blood bestie, or an online 'friend'?
A trip to see Santa in Lapland or at the local department store?
Astroturf, or lush Wembley grass?
Monopoly money, or real cash?
A fake smile, or a heartfelt grin?

There's more but I'm hoping the penny is beginning to drop.

Okay, it's not totally clear cut. Fake lashes and nails ... they're designed to make you look better than the original. And your selfie might actually look more attractive if you let the filter work its magic?[2]

But generally speaking, the real thing is nearly always better than the cheaper or fake alternative. Think about it, would you rather have a genuine Van Gogh hanging on your bedroom wall, or a £10 print off the internet?

Real or fake? The difference is priceless!
My point is that there are a lot of things that you can fake in life. In fact, you can almost fake life itself. Which brings me back to the original question: *What kind of person do you want to be when you grow up?*

I want to be real. I want to be *authentically* me. Chances are, you want to be authentically you.

The bare-knuckled truth? It's easy to pretend to be somebody you're not. It's even easier to live as a pale imitation of yourself. It's easy to make excuses as to why your life hasn't turned out quite as you hoped.

It's easy to settle for 'fine'.

The Art of Being Brilliant is about raising your wellbeing bar to mental WEALTH by getting good at being you. Get good at being you and you'll raise the bar from mental health to mental WEALTH. But that means no more fakery, no more pale imitation and no more settling for 'that'll do'.

No more excuses!

---

2 For the record, I'd argue *very strongly* that the raw selfie is way more gorgeous than the airbrushed nonsense, and your actual real lashes are lush enough.

Andy and I are super-excited to have you aboard. Now sign the contract below and let's get cracking.

♥Life The official contract.

Available for a limited time only.
Limit 1 (one) per person.
Cats are special, they get nine.
NO rehearsals allowed.
Subject to change without notice.
Life can have ↓ downs as well as ups ↑.

NO warranty, refunds or do-overs.
Banana skins guaranteed.
fairness NOT included.
Sole responsibility of the user.

#Special

BEST BEFORE DEATH

Signature: ....

#ArtOfBrillBook #YOLO #YODO #4000weeks #NoMoreExcuses

THREE: Shiny HAPPy people

Brace yourself for a complicated formula, a fast-flowing river and two decades of reverse psychology.

You're introduced to a recurring theme of the book – the so-called two-percenters – and then spend a couple of paragraphs luxuriating in the benefits. Oh, and if you've ever wondered how much love actually costs, we have the answer to that, too.

But first, 'Doctor, doctor, I feel like a pair of curtains ...'

'Doctor, doctor ...'

Maybe you've heard the story of the man who went to see an eminent Viennese psychiatrist, complaining that, for some reason, he felt sad all the time. After some discussion, the doctor said, 'Let me suggest, as a first step, that you go to the theatre tonight. The great clown Grimaldi is performing here in Vienna. He is so funny, he makes everyone laugh.'

'But Doctor', sighed the patient, *'I am Grimaldi!'*

It's a lovely story that holds an important truth. Nobody's happy ALL the time. Sadness is an important part of life. It's okay NOT to be okay. Painting a fake smile on your face is NOT the answer.

Upgrading to 'best self' is a BIG part of the answer. Once you have purpose, meaning, positivity, gratitude and strong relationships, a lot of the low-level dreariness melts away.

No, you won't have a smile on your face and a spring in your step all the time, *just more of the time*

Rocket science

There are some seriously clever people out there. I once got an email from an academic who had so many letters after her name that I thought she might have had a stroke and collapsed on her keyboard!

I doff my cap to the heavyweights, but personally, I'm a big fan of *simplifying* their academic hieroglyphics.

Here's an example. Researchers at University College London spent a load of time and money researching the secrets of happiness and, guess what, they did exactly what you'd expect scientists to do. They justified their research paper by creating a formula.

You ready for it?

Please imagine a drum roll ... while I reveal what humans have been searching for since time began – the secret formula for happiness, according to UCL[3]

... is this ...

$$\text{Happiness}(t) = w_0 + w_1 \sum_{j=1}^{t} y^{t-j} CR_j + w_2 \sum_{j=1}^{t} y^{t-j} EV_j + w_3 \sum_{j=1}^{t} y^{t-j} RPE_j$$

$$+ w_4 \sum_{j=1}^{t} y^{t-j} \text{Max}(R_j - O_j, 0) + w_5 \sum_{j=1}^{t} \text{max}(O_j - R_j, 0)$$

You'll most likely be scratching your head in befuddlement and thinking what I'm thinking – *what the heck's all that about?*

If you unpick the formula it basically suggests that you should lower your expectations of happiness, and that way, you'll never be disappointed.

I have several issues with the formula. First, they seem to have confused it with rocket science; second, it's wrong (why on earth

---

3 If you're struggling (which I know you absolutely are) the equation is best explained at Phys.org: https://phys.org/news/2016-06-happiness-equation-reveals-people-fortunes.html

would you go through life with such low expectations?); and the third, the secret of happiness doesn't require a complicated formula at all.

For those who like simple science, read on ...

Reverse Psychology

I'm a rotcod. That's 'doctor' backwards! I'm basically the exact opposite of all the other doctors you've ever met.

I'm not a medical doctor. I can't whip your appendix out and please don't ask me to look at your rash or the fungus between your toes.

I'm a Doctor of Positive Psychology. Let me explain ...

Since its birth in the 1800s, the subject of psychology has largely been a 'disease model'. It's predicated on illness. Most psychologists study disorders – anxiety, depression, phobias, trauma – those kinds of things. This makes perfect sense because once someone from the medical profession has diagnosed you with something they can apply therapy, counselling or meds to help you.

Psychology exists for the right reasons. 'Fixing' people is an incredibly noble and very useful thing to do.

But (and it's a big BUT) despite the combined efforts of the psychological profession – 150 years of administering the best therapy and medication that we can concoct – the truth is that mental ill health has been getting steadily worse, not better!

Look around. Depression, anxiety, panic and stress ... they're all on an exponentially upward curve. It's incredibly common for people to be taking pills to combat the side-effects of the side-effects of medication they're taking for whatever the original problem was.

The median age of mental ill health is being lowered, meaning that more and more young people are succumbing to anxiety (and worse). At the time of writing this sentence, we're just short of 100 million antidepressant drugs being prescribed every year in the UK (that's way more than there are people), and by the time you read this sentence that figure will have climbed.[4]

The grimmest statistic of them all is that global suicide rates are close to a million people a year. The sobering reality is that one person is taking their own life every 40 seconds.[5]

My point? Despite the well-intentioned efforts of doctors, therapists and counsellors the truth is that mental ill health has skyrocketed. That's a big fat clue that the current approach might need a re-think.

'Depression is a lying b*****d. You'll have better days, I promise you.'

Sue Fitzmaurice. Author.

---

4 The numbers are impossible to pin down. My stats are taken from various sources: The breakdown is England 86 million, Scotland 3 million, Wales 3.2 million, NI 3.5 million. Indeed, Northern Ireland is described as a 'world leader' in prescription drug use.

5 World Health Organization https://www.who.int/news-room/fact-sheets/detail/suicide

The twelve best doctors in the world.

1. Outdoors
2. Rest
3. Exercise
4. Healthy diet (but with occasional cake)
5. Self-confidence ↖ mmm cake!
6. Friendship
7. Good quality sleep
8. Happiness
9. Love
10. Time
11. Play
12. Not taking yourself too seriously

A white-water life

Archbishop Desmond Tutu was a man with a twinkle in his eye. 'The Arch' and Mr Mandela were probably as influential a pair as the world has ever seen. Tutu used to tell the story of a man standing on the bank of a fast-flowing river. Above the sound of the torrent he heard someone yelling and he looked upstream to see a woman being carried by the current, arms waving, 'Help, help, I'm drowning!'

The man secured his life jacket and waded in, pulling the drowning woman to safety. As she coughed and spluttered in her recovery, the man heard another call for help and he waded in again, this time rescuing a teenager in trouble.

No sooner had the young person been pulled from the swirling water, there was a third, fourth and fifth drowning person.

At which point Desmond Tutu delivers the punchline like only Desmond Tutu can. He says there comes a point where we need to stop pulling people out of the water and go upstream to find out why they're falling in in the first place.

The Arch has beautifully articulated the difference between traditional strands of psychology (the noble art of rescuing people who are struggling) and positive psychology (equipping people with strategies so they are able to rescue themselves).

The therapy and counselling professions are overwhelmed by metaphorically yanking people out of the river. Upstream is where we need to be. There is a lot of 'white water' in the modern world. Positive psychology is about learning to be your own first responder.

The rise of the two-percenters

'Positive psychology' is a subject popularised by Professor Martin Seligman.[6] It's been around since the 1990s but the Prof. wouldn't claim to have invented the study of wellbeing and flourishing – they've been on the radar for centuries. Go way back and you'll have heard Plato and Confucius banging on about the good life. More recently, Carl Rogers, Howard Gardiner and the god of management courses the world over, Abe Maslow. All have elements of self-fulfilment, happiness and subjective wellbeing in their studies. So although it's hitting today's headlines, I guess positive psychology is best described as having a very short history with a very long past.

As hinted at earlier, there's a general acknowledgement that for its 150 years of existence psychology has been predicated at illness rather than wellness. The subject has developed branches, or specialisms, to deal with the various ailment offshoots. Excuse my pen portraits, but clinical psychology tends to be about easing mental suffering while developmental psychology often focuses on impairment of language or motor skills. Forensic psychology helps solve crimes and catch serial killers. Neuropsychology is often about brain disorders, educational psychology helps work out why children are struggling at school.

In short, you're very unlikely to be referred to a psychologist if you're buzzing with health, happiness and vitality!

Basically, if individuals lie on a range of wellbeing from −10 (very unwell) to +10 (very well indeed) then we've always been focused

---

6 Check him out at https://positivepsychology.com/who-is-martin-seligman/

on getting people from say minus 8, 9 or 10 to zero (to the point of them 'not being ill'). Job done! Except of course it isn't!

Positive psychology is about getting to a plus 8 or 9. In my research I describe this as 'flourishing'.

Fascinated by the positive end of the wellbeing spectrum, I decided to do the exact opposite of what most of the other psychologists were doing. My idea was this; what would happen if, instead of studying poorly people, we studied well people? So, instead of finding out what's wrong with you, we revealed what's right with you.

I surveyed a whole bunch of people to gauge how happy they were, and plotted them onto a wellbeing graph.[7] The hugely simplified cartoon version looks a little bit like this …

---

7 Again, for the purists, I'm at pains to point out that this diagram and the term 'two-percenters' doesn't appear in my PhD thesis. This book is about providing a hugely simplified summary that gives you the headline news, but without marinating you in the data. Therefore, if you're thinking 'It can't be THAT simple', you're correct. Reminder, the thesis is downloadable from www.artofbrilliance.co.uk

Broadly speaking, if we measure levels of happiness and wellbeing on the lollipop chart, most people in the developed world inhabit the 'perfectly fine' zone. We generally have reasonable health, a roof over our head, a fridge full of food and a comfy bed. In terms of happiness, most people are 'mildly happy most of the time'.[8]

However, this millennium has seen change accelerate to warp speed. Climate emergency, social media, technology, algorithms, neurodiversity, epidemics, pandemics, artificial intelligence, fake news, wars … in such challenging times, even those who were 'perfectly fine' have begun to run on empty and before you know it, low-level negativity has kicked in.

People who've been running on negative thoughts for a long time can slip into the danger zone. This is where the mental health alarm bells begin to sound and, fingers crossed, the professionals will step in and offer therapy, counselling or meds. As I said a few paragraphs ago, this is how the medical profession has operated *forever*. They wait for people to be ill, and then step in to rescue them.

For the record, I am not anti-traditional psychology. Diagnosing and helping people is absolutely the right thing to do.

BUT (and it's an even bigger BUT than last time) positive psychology is about those at the other end of the wellbeing graph – the handful of people that we can all think of who have something extra (positivity, energy, spring in their step, enthusiasm, passion for life …) I nickname them the 'two-percenters' on the basis that there aren't very many of them. The two-percenters spend more time towards the top end of the wellbeing chart and have been ignored by psychologists on the grounds of them 'not being ill'.

---

8 No, not *everybody*, all the time. But despite what you see on the news we remain a relatively well-fed and prosperous country.

I reverse-engineered psychology, flipping it on its head and coming at it from the top end of the wellbeing graph. The happy ones, the flourishing few, the statistical outliers, those who are genuinely living their best lives ... I wanted to know three things:

1. The people who are feeling amazing on a regular basis, *who the heck are they?*

2. What are they doing that allows them to flourish?

3. Most importantly, what can we learn from them that we can apply to ourselves so we have a better chance of achieving mental WEALTH?

Basically, I started my PhD for purely selfish reasons. It wasn't research it was *ME-search*! Those two-percenters who are in love with life, I wanted to be one!

The good news, even better news and truly fabulous news

There are three pieces of good news about being a two-percenter. First, and most obviously, being your 'best self' more of the time (which is essentially what a two-percenter is) will fundamentally change the rest of your life, at work and home.

There are very sound business reasons for nurturing a two-percenter culture. Think of all those 'extra-mile' behaviours that make your workplace buzz – strong relationships, high productivity, creativity, passion, world-class customer service – these tend to happen naturally when a team is operating at its best. In positive psychology we call it 'collective effervescence': there's a buzz, an aliveness, a vibrancy about the place. These are the days when work doesn't feel like 'work'.

But the benefits spread wider than the workplace. At a family level, this collective effervescence tends to pass from generation to generation. The #1 rule of parenting is that your children will not do what you say, *but they will do what you do!* No pressure, but that means being a two-percenter at home is probably the most important thing you will ever do!

On a societal level, happy people live longer, have fewer ailments, are more altruistic, have more friends and make other people feel great too!

Second, my research points to the fact that upgrading to 'best self' is actually a set of learned behaviours. The two-percenters are not feeling brilliant by accident. Their amazingness comes from a set of habits, which in the cold light of day, turn out to be simple principles that, when applied, will nudge you in the right direction.

Third, and best news of all, there are tremendous side effects of feeling amazing. Human emotions are contagious so when you're functioning at your best, you create an emotional uplift in those around you. So sure, being a two-percenter is good for you, but it also spills out into your family, friends, work colleagues, neighbours and community.

But before I go any further, it might be worth stopping for a minute to reflect on you and your life. Concentrating on the positive end of the wellbeing graph – the two-percenters, the happy few, the ones who shine – who the heck are they?

Remember, you have been criticising yourself for years and it hasn't worked. TRY approving of yourself and see what happens.

Louise L. Hay

Author and self-help fairy godmother

Activity: Who's who?

A) Who are the stand-out people in your life (not celebs, I'm asking you to think about family, friends, co-workers, neighbours) and why do they stand out?

_____

_____

_____

_____

_____

B) Describe yourself in two-percenter mode. Be specific. What do you look, sound and feel like at your best?

_____

_____

_____

_____

In Part A, the chances are that the reason you chose your two-percenters as two-percenters is because when they're around, you feel great too. This is the acid test which brings me back to my thesis, and the word flourishing.

Which bleeds into Part B. That means that you, in two-percenter mode, will create an emotional uplift in those closest to you.

What price love?

Just so you know, at the time of writing this book, the cost of raising a child to the age of 18 is £223,356.[9] That's the basic, no-frills, heating, clothes and food price. If we add in luxuries such as toys, haircuts, holidays, games consoles and private education, it's eye-watering.

Kids are a big ticket item, which is why evolution created a chemical called oxytocin. Commonly called the love drug, oxytocin bonds families together. If it wasn't for oxytocin, there would be no human reproduction!

The love drug makes you forget about the £200-grand bill!

But here's our fun way of teaching your kids about the cost of living. Maybe leave the book lying around on the kitchen table, casually open, on the next page. ...

#ArtOfBrillBook #Grimaldi #ReversePsychology #2pecenter

9 *Huffington Post,* reporting on a MoneyFarm study https://www.huffingtonpost.co.uk/entry/the-cost-of-raising-a-child-in-2023_uk_64aea427e4b0e5efaadf7756

GIVE THE GIFT OF LIFE

Available for pre-order.
Best-seller. HUMAN BABY

All HUMAN BABY varieties come pre-programmed with unconditional love and arrive in rapid learning mode. **HUMAN BABY** can be programmed to speak any language. Adaptable to most environments. **HUMAN BABY** can be trained to walk and talk within ONE year and toilet trained in two years (models vary).

Several skin tones to choose from. HUMAN BABY comes in traditional girl and boy models, or our brand new non-binary edition.

HUMAN BABY comes factory fitted with cuteness. Special features; chubby cheeks, gurgling and dribbling.
Order your HUMAN BABY today and get these extras:

Sleep mode

Awake mode

Cry mode

Cry-for-no-reason mode

Wake at 3 am mode

Nappy-filling mode

Projectile-vomiting mode

Available in various sizes. Standard delivery is nine months, but small ones can arrive early.

Starter price: £223, 356
No refunds. No warranty. No questions asked. No training required. Luxuries (haircuts, toys, education, etc.) not included.

(Please leave a note if you're not in and we can leave **HUMAN BABY** with a neighbour)

FOUR:
The curse of mediocrity

BEWARE of the Garbage Trucks...

...they're everywhere!!

It's all about positive thinking, right?

Wrong! We enlist legendary motivational speaker Zig Ziglar to help us explain.

This chapter has a bit of everything, from garbage trucks to destination addiction and botheredness. It's a scratch and sniff section ... nose in the air, deep breath, can you smell the whiff of a wellbeing revolution?

Start every day off with a smile and get it over with

W. C. Fields. American actor and comic.

Beware of the Garbage Trucks

The previous chapter had me atop my high psychological horse, extolling the reasons why being your best self is the right thing to do. I've argued that it'll change your life for the better, with the glow spreading to those you love. Which begs the question, *Why are there not more two-percenters?* Why is it that you can only think of a handful of these people, with the majority stuck in drudgery mode?

Here's a clue from David Pollay.[10] He's given me permission to use his exact words. This is what he learned in the back of a New York City taxi cab ...

I hopped in a taxi, and we took off for Grand Central Station. We were driving in the right lane when all of a sudden, a black car jumped out of a parking space right in front of us. My taxi driver slammed on his brakes, the car skidded, the tyres squealed, and at the very last moment our car stopped just one inch from the other car's back end.

I couldn't believe it. But then I couldn't believe what happened next. The driver of the other car, the guy who almost caused a big accident, whipped his head around and he started yelling bad words at us. And for emphasis, he threw in a one-finger salute, as if his words were not enough.

---

10 Top man. Check out his website https://www.davidpollay.com/

But then here's what really blew me away. My taxi driver just smiled and waved at the guy. And I mean, he was friendly. So, I said, 'Why did you just do that? This guy could have killed us!' And this is when my taxi driver told me what I now call, 'The Law of the Garbage Truck'.

He said, 'Many people are like garbage trucks. They run around full of garbage, full of frustration, full of anger and full of disappointment. As their garbage piles up, they look for a place to dump it. And if you let them, they'll dump it on you. So when someone wants to dump on you, don't take it personally. Just smile, wave, wish them well, and move on. Believe me. You'll be happier.'

So I started thinking, how often do I let Garbage Trucks run right over me? And how often do I take their garbage and spread it to other people at work, at home, or on the street? It was then I made a personal commitment and said, 'I don't want their garbage and I'm not going to spread it anymore.'

I began to see Garbage Trucks. Like in the movie *The Sixth Sense*, the little boy said, 'I see dead people.' Well now I see Garbage Trucks. I see the load they're carrying. I see them coming to dump it. And like my taxi driver, I don't take it personally. I just smile, wave, wish them well, and I move on.

Well said, that man!

In my research, I call it languishing but garbage trucks, mood hoovers, energy vampires, dementors ... call them what you want. To be clear, I'm not talking about people with clinical issues, I'm talking about people who are stuck in grumble mode, and who can expertly skewer you with a negative remark that drags you down to their level.

Work colleagues, friends or very close family members, I find myself wishing I had Netflix's 'Skip Intro' button, but for conversations. Your mood hoovers are people who light up the room, *when they leave!*

It can sometimes seem like Garbage Trucks are coming at you from every angle. You can almost hear the *beep, beep, beep* as they reverse towards you, ready to dump their detritus.

Mood hoover definition:

He has well and truly earned his place among our community's outstanding non-achievers.

If there's something missing in your life, it's probably **YOU!**

But one of my biggest epiphanies of all time is that, sometimes, *I am that lorry!* Understanding that, and realising it's the truth, is super-important because then, *and only then,* can I cease trying to fix other people, and start to fix myself.

Languishing is a sense that something's missing in your life and, guess what, that missing thing is YOU (at your best).

Here's an example from real life. I used to share an office with 'Michelle' (that may or may not be her real name) who, in the two-and-a-half years I sat next to her, had a one word catchphrase – 'nightmare!' That was pretty much it. She'd slope into the office in the morning, rolling her eyes because she had better things to do than come to work.

'How was your weekend Shell?'

'Don't ask', she'd retort. *'Nightmare!'*

Michelle wasn't anxious or depressed, merely a bit stuck. In Shell's world the weather was always too cold, rainy, hot, windy – too

something! Never brilliant. The phone would ring and she'd sigh. 'Phone's ringing again. That'll be a customer. *Nightmare!*'
This is how stuck Shell became. She eventually settled down and found a decent partner to share her life with. They married and had a son. Michelle proudly brought the two-week-old newborn into the office so we could all grin and coo at the loveliness of her baby. She cradled her little boy in her arms and I couldn't help but have a huge grin on my face. Michelle had grown up. 'Shell', I exclaimed, beaming from ear to ear. 'You're a mum!'

'I know,' she grimaced, *'nightmare!'*

Why didn't Shell's demeanour and language demonstrate her joy at her good fortune? It brings me back to the word 'stuck'.

It's a sure bet that you know some mood hoovers. If you bought them flowers they would grumble about having to get a vase. If they won the lottery they would grumble it wasn't a rollover. If you saved their life they would grumble that they now have to carry on paying tax. The invisible downward magnetic forces are partly due to the evolution of the human species. Homo sapiens are pre-programmed to be cautious and pessimistic. We've evolved as a species because we're survivors, and we've survived because we've been cautious. Darwin's 'survival of the fittest' is quite closely aligned with 'survival of the most careful'. I call it 'defensive thinking'.

The curse of mediocrity is all around us. We learn to count down to the weekend in what Robert Holden calls 'destination addiction'. We're eager to hurry life along, towards something good that lies in the future. You might have a holiday coming up, proudly declaring, 'Only three weeks to go!' without realising you've accidentally snared yourself in the trap of wishing your life away.

Botheredness

Positive psychology doesn't say that the majority are depressed or sad, merely that too many people are a million miles away from feeling as great as they could.

Our natural habitat lies in the bottom third of the enthusiasm chart, and we visit the two-percenter heights occasionally. Almost at random.

But what if it wasn't random? What if you can take back some control?

In the interests of not pulling any punches, here it is, straight up. The biggest reason why most people are a million miles away from feeling brilliant is that it's *easier* to be negative. It takes no effort whatsoever to conform to 'normal', and if 'normal' means we gripe about the traffic, the latest restructure at work, the economy, the state of the national sports teams and the weather, then so be it. Humans are gregarious. We're pack animals. We have an overwhelming desire to fit in. If everyone else is set to low-level grumble mode then it seems totally logical to do the same.

Please compose yourself before reading the next sentence. Being a two-percenter isn't always the easiest choice to make. In the pervading gloom of a seemingly negative world, it's considerably more challenging to be upbeat, happy and positive. And because it's hard work and it takes practice, most people can't be bothered to do it for long enough for it to stick.

'What is to give light must endure burning.'
Victor Frankl.
Holocaust survivor

43

My message is, *get bothered.* Life isn't a fitting in game, it's a STANDING OUT game.

There's nothing more important that you'll ever do than spread positive, upbeat, energetic, passionate vibes. You'll feel better for it and, crucially, those around you will respond in a positive manner. I'm promising that if you learn to live in the upper reaches of your wellbeing spectrum, and then do it for the next 40 years, it will change your life.

Significantly!

You will get markedly different results in terms of relationships, career, happiness … just about everything you do will yield better results when you do it as a positive human being. But there's an even bigger challenge ahead. The real question is, over the next few decades, how many people can you take with you? How many people can you influence in a positive way? How many can you inspire?

Nose to the air, I can sniff a wellbeing revolution!

'I count myself lucky, having long ago won a lottery paid to me in seven sunrises a week for life.'

Robert Brault. Writer.

Personal Q&A

What would you do if the world was going to end one week from today?

_____

_____

_____

_____

_____

Jump ahead to the end of your working life. Reflect back on your career. What are the three most important lessons you've learned and why are they so critical?

_____

_____

_____

_____

_____

Think of someone who inspires you. What exactly do they do that makes you feel so brilliant?

_____

_____

_____

_____

_____

Who are you at your BEST?

_____

_____

_____

_____

_____

It's your 100th birthday and there's a big family party in your honour. Someone is going to stand up and say a few words about you. What would you like them to say?

_____

_____

_____

_____

_____

List 10 things you really appreciate but that you take for granted.

_____   _____

_____   _____

_____   _____

_____   _____

_____   _____

What are the most IMPORTANT things to have emerged from answering these questions?

Slam dunk

Let's go back to those who inhabit the rarefied atmosphere of the upper reaches of the wellbeing chart. They're only human so they experience downtime, but their natural habitat is close to the top end of the wellbeing scale. They are experiencing elevated happiness and energy at levels of statistical significance. They're great to have around because they light up the room. So, that leaves us with the original questions … who the heck are they? What do they do that makes them so happy, and what can we learn from them that we can actually put into practice in our own lives?

It makes me smile when delegates on courses come up to me at break time and nod sagely. 'This is just about "positive thinking" isn't it? It's just glass-half-full stuff.' Absolutely not. Imagine you're taxiing on the runway about to take off on your holiday – here's an overly positive message you never want to hear. 'Good morning everybody. This is your captain speaking. Welcome aboard your flight to Palma Mallorca. Air traffic control have said it's too foggy to take off and we're only a quarter refuelled, but do you know what, I'm a two-percenter so I'm gonna give it a go.'

Noooooooo! Anything taken to the extreme, even positivity, is dangerous.

I cringed when I observed a session in a school where the trainer whipped the teenagers into a frenzy of thinking they could be whatever they wanted. They all whooped with joy as they stated their ambition. We had dozens of astronauts, professional footballers and brain surgeons.

There's nothing wrong with ambition and dreaming big. In fact, I actively encourage it (see the later chapter on huge goals).

But *The Art of Being Brilliant* isn't really about positive thinking. It's much more subtle than that. Zig Ziglar sums it up well in the following passage ...

'To be candid, some people have given positive thinking a bad name. I can't stand to hear some gung-ho individual say that with positive thinking you can just do "anything".

If you think about that one for a moment, you recognise the absurdity of it. As a ridiculous example, I'm a positive thinker, but I could never slam-dunk a basketball or perform major surgery – or even minor surgery – on anyone and expect that person to survive. Nate Newton, the 300-plus pound lineman for the Dallas Cowboys, is positive, optimistic and outgoing but he'd be a complete failure as a jockey or a ballet dancer.

It's safe to say that positive thinking won't let you do "anything". However, it is even safer to say that positive thinking will let you do "everything" better than negative thinking will. Positive thinking will let you use the ability which you have, and that is awesome. It works this way. You can walk into a dark room, flip on the switch and immediately the room is lighted. Flipping the switch did not generate the electricity; it released the electricity which had been stored. Positive thinking works that way – it releases the abilities which you have.'

Zig, I salute you!

Before I move on to some 'how tos', it's worth hammering the big finding from my PhD: being a two-percenter is about adopting a set of learned behaviours. To be clear – the upward journey from the 'curse of mediocrity' to the two-percenter zone – this 'best self' thing – doesn't tend to happen by accident. You learn it.

And, personally, I can't think of anything more important that you'll ever learn.

#ArtOfBrillBook #GarbageTrucks #Botheredness

'Son, if you really want something in this life, you have to work for it. Now quiet! They're about to announce the lottery numbers.'

Homer Simpson. Legendary cartoon dad.

FIVE:
Can God do a handstand?

I'm guessing, perhaps wrongly, that you'd like to be introduced to one of the laws of thermodynamics? Steering quickly through entropy and grinagogs, we reveal what's absolutely NOT making the evening news.

From then on it's rose tinted, all the way to Sheffield.

An introduction to the macroscopic perspective of classical thermodynamics

Just kidding. Here's the simple version …

There's a term from thermodynamic physics, 'entropy': it's the lack of order or predictability and describes the gradual decline into disorder. In straightforward language, it states that any machine, if left alone, will lose energy. It just seeps away! Therefore new energy has to be applied.

Entropy is this 'new energy'.

I'll give you an example from 1974. My dad used to have an old Vauxhall Viva. He bought a new car (a green Austin Maxi … nice move Pa!) and never sold the Viva. Every year it sat on the drive, rusting, losing its lustre. It started out shiny red and gradually turned dull pinky orange. The tyres went flat. It even developed a dent in its bumper, all of its own accord. My dad's Viva was the principle of entropy in action. It wasn't going anywhere. It wasn't being maintained so its energy just seeped away. In the end the scrap man gave my dad a tenner and away it went.

Bear with me … because entropy also applies to people and businesses.

Imagine energy measured on a scale of 0 to 10 where 0 is dead and 10 is you on a crazed-up, manic energy explosion. A lot of people seem to be at the 2, 3 or 4 end of the spectrum. Symptoms include a heavy heart on Monday, lethargy, counting down to the weekend and using your evenings to recover from work. What if we could raise you to the 7, 8, 9 end of the spectrum? That's where the two-percenters reside. There's a series of technical terms we use for this like 'alive', 'energetic', 'upbeat' and 'positive'. The symptoms include happiness, vigour, creativity, vivacity and a willingness to create and take opportunities. These great feelings are bigger than you, meaning that they leak out of you and create upward emotional spirals in the people around you (this is the flourishing effect that I was looking for in my research).

There is of course a fine line between this ideal state and a 10. It's perfectly possible to buzz around like a blue-arsed fly and be upbeat to the point of upsetting people with your positivity. Yes, you can be too happy. Toxic positivity is a thing!

If you wake up one morning to find your house has burned down, your partner has left you and the dog is dead, the last thing you need is someone saying, 'Every cloud … one door closes … plenty more fish in the sea …'.

Grinagog is a fabulous 17th-century word that describes someone who's so happy you want to punch them on the nose. I'm not recommending jazz hands, pretense or a fake smile. Plus, I'm also not advocating happiness and positivity always and forever … just a bit more often.

I don't want you off the scale, grinning inanely at people. Just up a notch or two (or maybe even three or four?). The point is startlingly simple. If you can increase your energy, you'll be more effective in these crazy times. My dad's Viva represents some of the people we've met over the years!

'Corporate entropy' is when organisations and teams run out of energy. *Literally!* Check out the following list. These are the indicators of 'corporate entropy' – sure signs that business energy is seeping away:

• There is no longer time for celebration.
• Problem makers outnumber problem solvers.
• Teams 'over-communicate' and 'under-converse' (for example, you email the person sitting next to you and copy in 65 people from across the organisation).
• The pressures of day-to-day operations push aside our concern for vision and creativity.
• Too many people have that 'here-we-go-again' feeling.
• People speak of customers as impositions on their time rather than opportunities to serve.
• The focus is on surviving the week.
• There's an emphasis on systems rather than people.

Kim Cameron's work on organisational vitality examines four types of energy; physical, mental, psychological and relational – only one of which is renewable.

Physical energy is the body's naturally occurring energy, produced by burning calories. Psychological energy is specifically to do with mental concentration and brain work. Emotional energy is all about experiencing intense feelings and is depleted by, for example, periods of intense excitement or sadness.

But it's the last one that's the biggy. *Relational* energy, in contrast to the other three, is an energy that increases as it is exercised. This form of energy is enhanced and revitalised through positive interpersonal relationships. Cameron describes relational energy as uplifting, invigorating and rejuvenating concluding it to be 'life-giving rather than life-depleting' (p. 51).[11]

11 Cameron, K. (2013). *Practicing Positive Leadership: Tools & Techniques that Create Extraordinary Results.* Berrett-Koehler.

Read that again because it's massive. Life-giving!

When you're in best-self mode you are breathing life into yourself and those around you. That sounds like worthwhile work.

The glow

For younger readers, there was a Ready Brek advert in the 1980s with the strapline, 'Central Heating for Kids'. The scene is a warm kitchen, with snow falling outside, as a young lad scrapes the last bits of hot oaty breakfast cereal from his bowl. The boy develops a rather strange orange glow on the outside and then dons hat and coat to go to play with his buddies in the snow. They've not had their Ready Brek, so our hero stands out a mile, his effervescence lighting up the winter scene. He's happier, more positive and warmer than the rest.

YouTube it. That advert is a great metaphor for entropy. You can see, hear and feel the difference! On the energy scale, his mates are a 3 and he's a 9.

> 'I have a new philosophy. I'm only going to dread one day at a time.'
>
> Charles M. Schultz Creator of Charlie Brown and Snoopy.

Which begs the question, how do we do it? How do we generate (and retain) a metaphorical glow on the outside when the news is so damned negative, your work colleagues are stuck in doom mode, the weather's rubbish and work pressures are massive.

It seems society is deliberately forcing us into a negative state. Watching the news is like being cornered by a pack of rabid dogs. It's a loop of disasters, poverty, corruption, famine, war, storms, fires, melting icecaps, bent politicians, tax rises, infidelities, enquiries, murders, bombings, depression, migrants, failing hospitals, recession, inflation and celebrity divorces.

So here's something that's a bigger deal than it sounds. Something conspicuous by its absence. When did you last see a crowd so happy that they organised a demonstration? It takes some imagining, but give it a go. Picture a swarm of smiley people in central London with banners proclaiming,

'My life is A⁺mazing'
'Thanks for the infrastructure'
'What a superb country'
'I ♥ life'

Have you ever heard a reporter standing outside a maternity unit babbling that, 'This hospital is working so brilliantly that the government has commissioned an independent review to find out why it's so epic. The aim is to share its sheer epicness across the NHS.'

To my knowledge, there's never been a petition handed in to 10 Downing Street with 100,000 names of people saying how content they are with their lot.

Yes, my examples are facetious but the point is valid – there's a news blackout on millions of citizens going about their honest days, working hard, coming home to their families, eating lovely food and then climbing into their comfy beds and sleeping soundly in their safe neighbourhoods.

All of the above is literally NOT breaking news!

Sure, it's happening, in towns and cities up and down the country, but is crowded out by deviations from the norm. The angry people, chronic illness, unsafe neighbourhoods, empty tummies, poor performing hospitals and failing schools – that what grabs the airtime.[12]

If you choose to do so, you can have this beamed into your life 24/7. It's a relatively new avenue of research but several studies have found that heavy news consumption can result in higher acute stress for the viewer than the people in the actual news![13]

Neuroscience suggests that you get what you focus on so if you're intent on fighting off the rabid dogs of doom I'd recommend that you do yourself a favour and consume a bit less news. In culinary terms, you need to be dipped in news, but not marinated.

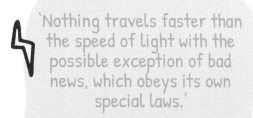

'Nothing travels faster than the speed of light with the possible exception of bad news, which obeys its own special laws.'

Douglas Adams. Best author ever.

---

12 I am absolutely not suggesting the world is perfect. I have both feet in the real world. Bad stuff exists, and it's very real. I'm merely reminding you that the news's job is to report deviations from the norm.

13 Example: Holmana, E.A., Garfin, D. and Cohen Silver, R. (2014). Media's role in broadcasting acute stress following the Boston Marathon bombings. Proceedings of the National Academy of Sciences of the United States of America, 111(1): 93–98.

May your life be as awesome as you pretend
it is on Facebook.

Guess what?

Here's a blog that I put out recently. It's making the same point in a slightly different way. Remember, your attention is precious, which is why the tech industry lures you in with clickbait.

If you're scanning every moment, looking for the bad, you'll find it. Because that's what you've programmed yourself to look for.

If you're scouring every face for evidence that you're not enough, you'll find it. Because that's what's in your personal search engine.

If you're endlessly scrolling, you'll find evidence of other people living seemingly perfect lives, and you'll feel inferior, or jealous. Because you've played the comparison game.

If you're devouring the news, you'll think the world's gone to hell in a handcart, because that's what you're consuming.

But can you see that the connection is YOU, and the filters you apply?

Personally, I figure that I can't change the world. But I can change mine. *And that means you can change yours!*

My positive psychology research is not happy-clappy. I'm not advocating rose-tinted Ray-Bans. In fact, quite the opposite. My role is to help you learn to clean the sh*t from your existing lenses.

We're NOT advocating rose - tinted Ray- Bans.

Look differently and see clearly, because guess what ...

Scan every moment for what's good, and you'll see it. Hidden in plain sight.

Scour every face for evidence of wonderful people, and you'll find them.

Feel lucky and grateful.

Quit the comparison game and you'll feel lucky. And grateful.

Switch off the news and look up. The world will seem more peaceful because that's what you're attending to.

If you look for the beautiful, for a solution, for the positive, then you've won at life. That's not rose-tinted. *It's true!*

Meanwhile, somewhere on the M1, just North of Sheffield ...

Here's an encounter between my co-author and his young daughter.

Liv is the light of my life, the joy in my heart, the inspiration in my soul and more often than not, the pain in my behind. I remember a conversation we had, when she was no older than four. Travelling back from my parents in Morecambe, on the M1 just north of Sheffield (that's a nice run in the car, you should do it one Sunday), it went like this:

Olivia: 'Father darling.' (She is very well spoken for someone born in Mansfield.)

Andy: 'What?' (I'm not very well spoken for someone born in Morecambe.) I replied, whilst noticing her in the rear view mirror looking out of the back window towards the sky.

Olivia: 'Did God make the sky Daddy?' she asked with a real look of curiosity on her face.

Andy: 'Yes, God made the sky' (nodding wisely, but not entirely convinced, trying to reconcile the whole 'Old Testament' with the 'Big Bang' conundrum).

Olivia: 'Can I make the sky Daddy?' she asked.

Andy: (chuckling knowingly) 'Probably not, sweetheart.'

Olivia: 'Did God make the birds, Daddy?' she asked, still looking out of the car window.

Andy: 'Yes, darling. God probably did make the birds.'

Olivia: 'Can I make the birds?'

Andy: 'Probably not, darling.'

We went back and forth: mountains, oceans, grass – she would ask me whether God made them and I had to inform her that yes, He did, and that she couldn't. All the time she was looking more and more confused about the fact that God could create all these wonderful things and she couldn't. I was thinking where the heck has this conversation come from, and probably more importantly, where was it heading?

Olivia paused for a minute and I breathed a sigh of relief. Maybe she'll change the subject, I hoped. It was then that she posed the killer WHY question …

Olivia: 'Why Daddy? Why can God make those things and I can't?'

I thought long and hard as I didn't want to give her a standard adult reply such as 'Just ... because' or, even worse, 'Go and ask your mum.' I came up with something that I'm proud of to this very day.

Andy: 'Sweetheart, God made all those things so you don't have to. They are already here for you to enjoy, so you can focus on what it is you want to achieve with your life.'

Have that! Quite a heavy answer for a four-year-old, but I have always thought you should speak to children as real people.

Olivia (quick as a whip): 'Can God do a handstand?'

(To be continued ...)

#ArtOfBrillBook #Entropy #ReadyBrek #CanGodDoAHandstand

SIX: You're toast.

A true story about a toaster

An eclectic chapter that includes Spike Milligan, Nina Simone, teeth and kidneys.

But settle yourself in for the centrepiece, a story that contains toasters, hospital wards, sick bowls, umbilical cords and miniature toes.

First up, insanity ...

Teeth and kidneys

Andy and I need to come clean here. We're not religious, as in, we don't adhere to a set of organised beliefs and practices. Please don't hold it against us but mosques, temples, synagogues and churches aren't our thing.

Spirituality on the other hand ... in the sense of being connected to a sense of peace, purpose, self, others and 'now' ... is something that continues to creep up on us as we mature.

For me, it kickstarted when I read a book on mindfulness in which there was a wonderful piece of advice – *wake up every morning and be grateful you've not got toothache.* A bit bizarre when I read it but I actually did that every single day for a whole year. Note, being grateful that my teeth aren't hurting is not an accidental thought. I'm unlikely to randomly think it at 6 am on a cold dark February morning. I would have to make an effort to consciously think it, which I did, 365 days on the bounce.

Picture the scene. The alarm beeps at stupid o'clock. I poke a toe out from under the duvet and it shoots back undercover. *Too early. Too dark. Too cold.* I slowly come to consciousness. Another day. Same old routine. *But wait!* My hand strokes my jaw. *No toothache. Yippee! What an awesome start to the day!*

The awareness that *I haven't* got toothache means I leap out of bed, energised, and ready for action. Sounds daft? Try it, it works. And it's not really about toothache. The principle is very profound.

Thank God (or your lucky stars, depending on your belief system) that you can get out of bed at all.

Every morning, appreciate that you don't have toothache and that your kidneys are working. Understand that the **average** lifespan is 4000 weeks and **one** day you won't be able to get out of bed (sounds harsh, **but** it's true). Being able to get out of bed is the **best** thing ever.

When was the last time you thanked your kidneys? Or your heart for pumping all that glorious oxygenated blood? Or your ears or tastebuds? Wow, we're lucky people! As soon as you start to attach a value to your health you will immediately feel more energetic. If life is a short and precious gift, it makes sense to appreciate it. Being alive is the best thing ever!

'I opened two gifts this morning. They were my eyes.'

Zig Ziglar.
Motivational speaker.

The ToM2000 story

My old toaster went kaput in January. It was a wedding gift so I've got no experience of ever purchasing a toaster. I drove to a soulless, out-of-town shopping centre and purchased a brand spanking new toaster, their top of the range Toast-o-Matic 2000 (four slices, brushed silver, cruise control, the works).

I got the ToM2000 home and unpacked it. She's a beauty, gleaming and aerodynamic, not like the old, green two-slicer that had given up on us.

Before I started experimenting with my sleek new bread cooking machine, I noticed it came with an instruction booklet. I'm not normally the type who goes in for instructions, but this time it was different. I clutched the booklet and made for my favourite chair. I was feeling warmhearted, possibly elated by my purchase. Somebody had spent time writing this booklet and I was determined to read it. I owed it to them. I turned the pages.

Twelve languages, *impressive!*

I decided to just read the English. Found it. The first four pages were health and safety. Apparently toast can be very dangerous. It's basically very hot bread, so be careful out there, everybody. Don't stick a fork in the toaster or use the ToM2000 while you're in the bath. Sensible advice if, I may say, a little over-cautious.

Eventually I found the actual instructions on how to make toast and I'd like to share it with you. Ready? Here goes …
I. Insert bread (or muffin, bagel, etc.)
II. Turn knob to the colour you want it
(from snow white to carbon black)

III. Push the lever down (unless you're in the bath, remember?)
IV. Wait
V. Toast pops up
VI. Remove cooked bread, apply butter, jam, etc. and scoff it.

Twelve languages! Someone's put an awful lot of work into that toaster manual. Hang in there; this will make sense in a minute …

Please rewind to 11th May 1995. I was about to become a dad. My wife was in Derby Royal Hospital and I was stroking her forehead. Twenty-four hours later I'm still stroking her forehead and there's no baby. They've given her some drugs to help move things on but my wife is stuck at three inches dilation. The baby's not for birthing.

Quite suddenly, Louise's blood pressure spikes, her ankles swell and within 10 minutes she's being wheeled into theatre for a caesarean. I jump at the chance to come along in an observing capacity. Even better, I get dressed up in green surgeon gear, mask and gloves – the full doctors' and nurses' fancy dress.

It's an epidural so Louise is awake, but numb from the waist down. My duties included wafting her with a sick bowl, with the added responsibility of commentating on what's happening at the action end. The surgeons went about their work. Five minutes and a small incision later, a very small scrap of a child is pulled from Lou's tummy (have you seen *Alien*?).

Thankfully, these are professional people. Cords are cut, the slime wiped off the infant and it's handed to me. I'm a dad. Six weeks earlier than expected too! There are hearty congratulations from all the team and then they abandon me and my newborn and return to the lady with big ankles. There's poking, prodding and stitching to be done.

I'm left, literally, holding the baby. The as yet unnamed baby girl weighs in at a tiny four-and-a-half pounds. It's an emotional moment. Father meets daughter for the very first time. I stared adoringly at my first born. And my first words, the momentous welcome to the world? 'It's got eyes!' I exclaimed as the tot stared up at me. My daughter was wrapped in a white towel with a tiny baby foot hanging out. 'And feet … *with miniature toes!'*

So, yes, terrible first words. I'm hoping my final words to her might be more profound? The point of my story is that there was no manual.

My Toast-o-Matic 2000 comes with health warnings and instructions in 12 languages when actually it's stupidly simple. Yet the most complex piece of kit on earth, a human life, comes with no instruction booklet. We have to make it up as we go along.

So, can I just explore this a tiny bit further: 11th May, I'm not a dad; 12th May, I am a dad. All of a sudden my life has changed. *Dramatically.* I have a tiny scrap of a human being, with huge eyes and lots of spare skin, who is entirely dependent on me (and her mum, to be fair).

Which brings me to a huge question that literally nobody is asking: *Who taught you how to think?*

Furrow your brow and rub your chin for a moment while you consider the question. Because I'd put it to you that nobody formally taught you how to think. Nobody ever actually sat you down and said, 'OK mate, this is how it's done. This is a thinking lesson.' There's no school exam in 'thinking'. You have to think to get the answers but 'thinking' isn't taught. In fact, we cram our children full of reading, maths, science, cooking, PE, French, geography and media studies, yet the most important piece of kit – their brain – remains a mystery.

So, if nobody actually taught you to think, where did your thinking come from?

Again, in the interests of plain speaking, *you made it up!* You kind of learned it via osmosis. When you were tiny, your parents and guardians had a way of thinking that they imbued upon you. And then you went to school and met 30 other kids in your class and they all had a way of thinking. You wanted to fit in so you did what they did (not knowing that they were making it up as well) and your teachers imparted a way of thinking too (they were also making it up, albeit from a slightly more experienced vantage point). But the most crucial people in all of this were your parents.

So, if you're still with me, let's probe a little deeper. Who taught your *parents* how to think? That's right – *their* parents. And who taught your grandparents to think? Brilliant, you've got it. *Their* parents. And they got it from *their* parents, etc.

We've ended up with quite a fixed way of thinking, passed down to us through the generations. It has changed a little but the essence is exactly the same. Our way of thinking is inherited.

Keep an open mind on this next question, because it's ginormous. We've established that nobody actually taught you to think. If you consider all the thinking you've done

'My Father had a profound influence on me. He was a lunatic.'

Spike Milligan.
British comedian.

over your lifetime, and all the thinking that everyone on the planet's been doing, and consider this whopper:

What if we've been doing it wrong?

What if there was a better way? What if there was a way of thinking that freed you from the shackles of negativity that has pervaded generation after generation?

Good news, *there is!*

What if you could learn to think in a way that enhanced your energy, made you stand out in a crowd and became a habit that would change your life.

Do you want some even better news? *You can!*

Read on, your mental software upgrade awaits!

Famously, what Nina Simone DID have ...
I got my hair on my head
I got my brains, I got my ears
I got my eyes, I got my nose
I got my mouth, I got my smile
I got my tongue, I got my chin
I got my neck, I got my boobies
I got my heart, I got my soul
I got my back, I got my sex
I got my arms, I got my hands
I got my fingers, I got my legs
I got my feet, I got my toes
I got my liver, got my blood ...
Got life
I got my life!

#gratitude

I got my...
hair on my head
brains
Smile
nose
ears
neck
chin
eyes
Mouth
tongue
hands
arms
fingers
heart
soul
back
boobies
Sex
liver
legs
blood
feet
toes
Got life
I got my life!

BONUS OFFERING: The 3Rs

Relationships, relationships, relationships!!

Hang on a second, why does this chapter have no number, and why's it called a BONUS OFFERING?

Because it's about the 3Rs (relationships, relationships & relationships), that's why. It's about *people*, not numbers.

Nuff said.

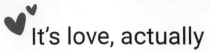
It's love, actually

Here's a challenge. I want you to organise these five things into priority order. No cheating or over-thinking, just total honesty.

In terms of importance to you (and they're all important!), how would you rank these five things:

Relationships. Success. Money. Happiness. Health.

1 _____

2 _____

3 _____

4 _____

5 _____

> 'Some people are worth melting for.'
> Olaf the Snowman, from Frozen.

I did the ranking activity with a bunch of 14-year-olds in Birmingham and they debated, argued and engaged. Some went for money as their priority ('Because sir, if I had money I could buy all the others') but most went for relationships, health or happiness.

We were about to move on when one of the lads raised his hand and said, 'Sir, you've missed something off the list.'

I looked at the five words emblazoned on the screen and then back at the lad with a furrowed brow. 'What do you mean?'

'Love, sir. If you add love to the list it changes everything.'

And 230 teenagers nodded in agreement. It's love, actually.

Some random phone stats[14]

The average person looks at their phone 150 times a day. There's a category of super-users who glance at their beloved screen 358 times a day.

71% of people check their phone as soon as they wake up (3% of people sleep with their phone in their hand and 15% with it under their pillow).

64% of people use their phone on the toilet (and a third of them have dropped their phone down the toilet, some more than once).

61% of people have texted someone in the same room as them.

48% feel panic/anxiety when their phone battery dips below 20%.

36% would rather give up their pet than their phone.

66% of people show signs of nomophobia (smartphone addiction).

52% of teenagers sit around in silence, staring at their phones, when they are together with friends.

10% of people look at their phone during sex (ahem, come on people!)

The average phone use is 2 hours and 54 minutes per day (which equals 44 days per year). Note, we average about 45 minutes of daily face-to-face contact with our families.

Could happen ...
Civilisation collapses.
Nobody looks up
from their phones.

14 Source: techinjury.net, business insider, reviews.org

Almost everything will work again if you unplug it for a few minutes.

Including you.

One moment in time

While you're digesting the smartphone stats, here's a BIG thought about FOMO and screen time. We're driven to our devices for fear of missing out when, of course, the ultimate irony is that we absolutely *are* missing out. On the moment. The only moment there ever is.

This moment.

I'm advising that you make yourself a priority and treat yourself to a smartphone detox. It's like kale for the mind.

Here's the clincher. In positive psychology there's something called Dunbar's number.[15] It means you spend about 40% of your life with a small group of between six and eight people. These are your very close family and friends.

Your tribe.

Another 20% of your time is spent with an additional slightly wider circle of half a dozen. If I cut to the chase, it boils down to this; you spend about 60% of your life with a dozen or so people.

It's worth pausing and thinking about your tribe. Who are your closest dozen?

Whoever they are, the science is clear. Although you might have 10,000 'friends' online – your wellbeing is much more likely to be linked to quality of your relationships with your closest dozen flesh and blood friends and family.

So it's worth giving you a few pointers about relationships and people.

---

15 Dunbar's number is neatly summarised in the *New Scientist*: https://www.newscientist.com/definition/dunbars-number/

I think many of us, if we slow down long enough to take a look at ourselves, don't give our relationships the time or attention necessary to keep them healthy and happy. We end up taking people for granted – especially those we love the most, which is kind of strange.

Paradoxically, in our hyper-connected world, more and more people are finding it harder to take the time to simply *be* with somebody else for a while. I'm talking eye contact, earphones out, with an actual real person.

Anyone can listen. All you have to do is take your earphones out, look up from your screen and stop talking! But to be a black belt listener you have to be genuinely interested in other people. Yes, *genuinely*! I call it 'listening with fascination' and it's a fabulous skill to develop. Listening with fascination is about being interested and asking follow-up questions.

I promise that if you're *genuinely* interested in other people, they'll think you're more interesting. I know, that's weird, right. Because it seems as though the more you talk about yourself, the more interesting you'll seem.

But, no, I'm afraid not.

Think about it … all the people you really like are interested in you, because, bingo, that's how it works.

Keep your questions positive. So instead of, 'How was your day?' try asking, 'What was the highlight of your day?', 'What's been the best thing about your day?' or 'What's gone well today?'

If you've got small children, try asking 'How was school: good, fantastic or brilliant?' Ask it consistently, with genuine enthusiasm, and you'll open them up to share the highlight of their day.

And when they share the good stuff, follow up with the best question ever, the one that will make YOU seem more interesting, which is simply this; 'Tell me more … .'

Then shush, listen and be *genuinely* interested. You have two ears and one mouth for a reason.

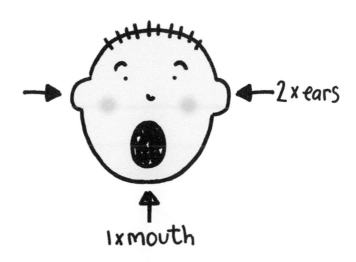

'**NEVER** worry what the cool people think. Head → for the **WARM** people. Life is **warmth**. You'll be cool when you're dead.'

Matt Haig, Author extraordinaire.

They're talking about you behind your back

I bet you didn't know there was an opposite to paranoia?

Which is pronoia … when people are saying *nice* things about you behind your back!

Imagine other people talking about you but saying how amazing you are, or how kind, or what a hard worker you are, or how proud they are.

Pronoia – two top tips spring from your new word. A relationship quick win is to say nice things about people, *behind their back.* To their face too, obviously, but there's something extra-special about saying nice things about people when they're not there. It seems to super-charge the niceness.

It's free and simple. Often, your nice comments will find their way back to the person you were talking about, which makes them feel amazing.

Of course, it's very easy to slip into the opposite. It's easy to gossip, pick fault or say nasty things about people behind their back.

So don't!

You can also extend the exact same rules to your online relationships. Remember it's called social media, not *anti*-social media so less doom scrolling, no nastiness and stop feeding the trolls. Instead of horrible comments just post good stuff; praise, encouragement, love, positivity, gratitude.

It won't stop other people being nasty, but you're not other people. You're you. It doesn't *matter what they're doing*, it matters what you're doing. It pays to be a lover, not a hater.

If you look at all the positive psychology research that's ever been done and do what's called a meta-analysis (that means you analyse lots of analysis until you get to analysis paralysis), you'll discover that the secret of happiness is in fact …

Relationships!

A real
friend
↓

↑
the flesh & blood type!!

I LOVE YOU

That will be all for today.

So, yes, the weather, money, purpose, attitude and gratitude all play a part in your happiness pie, but the biggest slice that's in your control is people. More specifically, your ability to stay socially connected to a team, tribe, clan, community or family.

If you listed the top 10 happiest *moments* of your life I'm almost certain that there won't be any products on there. Your happiest *moments* will be experiences, with people you love.

Plot spoiler, what goes around comes around, so be a giver, not a taker.
If you want more happiness, *be* happy
If you want more kindness, *be* kind.
If you want love, *be* loveable
If you want friendship, *be* a good friend
If people don't understand you, take steps to understand them *first*.
If people aren't nice, try being nice to them *first*.

On behalf of the world, thank you.

#ArtOfBrillBook #3Rs #Pronoia

SEVEN: Master Mind.
An instruction manual for your brain

Are the best chefs the ones who can cook a meal the fastest? Are the best authors the ones who can knock out a book the fastest? Are the best actors the ones who can deliver their lines the quickest? Are the best lovers the ones who can ...

Ahem! Speed isn't everything, so this chapter explores the busyness epidemic before segueing into deletion, distortion and generalisation. Along the way there are hidden giraffes, a few silly mind games, a to-be list and an awareness of Awareness Day.

Oh, and the ending? It's a funny thing, humour. What makes one person laugh will merely aggravate someone else. If your sense of humour remains intact, SEVEN has a great ending.

Your Swiss army phone

We all want to feel amazing, and yet most people are a million miles away from feeling as great as they could.

'Busyness' is a modern-day impediment. To be fair, the word's been around for a long time but 'busyness' has only recently kicked into modern parlance as a badge of honour.

'How are you?'

'Oh, you know, *keeping busy.*'

Busyness is an epidemic that's swept the world. I remember sitting in an Economics lecture in the late 1980s and learning that by the year 2000 we'd all have loads of spare time. Robots would be doing the work and people would be enjoying days of leisure. We'd be in the gym or on ocean cruises, with pots of money and nothing to do. It was billed as future bliss.

It's clear we were sold a pup. Leisure time? It's like the mythical thing they call a 'lunch hour'! Most people are working longer hours, not shorter ones. And life's got faster not slower. You email the person sitting next to you. You text your kids to tell them tea's ready.

#Fact

The queue to see the Mona Lisa is about an hour. The Louvre found that people looked at the world's most famous painting for 15 seconds, then turned their back, took a selfie and moved on.[16]

For anyone born today, tech is their first language. True story, I have a friend who's child's first word was Alexa!

Knowledge is at our fingertips. We no longer have to be smart because all the information in the world *ever* is available on your smartphone. It's no wonder you're addicted!
New relationship, swipe right.
New shoes? *Click*, next day delivery.
Set your podcast to play at 1.5 speed so you can listen quicker.
Camera, map, banking, music, films, social, calculator, meetings, torch, news, weather, tickets … it's a Swiss army phone.

Science and technology seem to have thought of everything, except how to make us all happy and contented.

I'm not suggesting any of this is necessarily wrong. The modern world is what it is. But here's a thought. Is it any coincidence that as the world has accelerated to cheek-wobbling speed, societal anxiety has mushroomed and attention spans shrunk? It's as though we are a human race in name and nature, lung busting our way through a 4000-week sprint, blinkered to a lot of the richness along the way.

If you want to wrestle back some control of your life, you have to find peace and contentment in the craziness. For me, that's not

16 *Huffington Post:* How Long Does it Take to Look at a Painting? https://www.huffpost.com/entry/how-long-does-it-taketo_b_779946#:~:text=The%20Louvre%20found%20that%20people,35%2C000%20works%20in%20the%20collection.

necessarily about slowing down for two weeks on holiday, it's about noticing the everyday moments that are always there, but that most people are too busy to notice.

Let me give you a very simple example:

I'm ashamed to say that I recently contributed a children's story for an anthology of *One Minute Bedtime Stories* for busy parents who don't have time to read a whole chapter. Reflecting on the project, I'm ashamed of myself for doing it. Even worse, when I knew the

book was coming out my initial reaction was 'great idea' because now I can get the bedtime story over with quickly.

In our house it had become a bit of a chore, especially with my son. I was always busy doing emails, writing or preparing for the next day's course and there'd be a tap at the kitchen door. 'Daddy, can you come and read me a bedtime story?'

'For heaven sake,' I'd sigh, 'you're 23. When are you going to start reading your own bedtime stories?' (Sorry, that's a cheap and probably not very funny gag, I'm talking about when he was about four or five).

I'd try to do the decent dad thing and read a bedtime story to my son. I'd sit on the end of Ollie's bed and go through the motions. I'd read quickly so I could get back to my emails. Sometimes I'd even miss a couple of pages out. The trouble is that Ollie's a bright lad and he knew when I was missing bits out. So he'd tell me, I'd deny it; we'd end up arguing because he wanted the proper version and I wanted the speedy version! I'd end up finishing in super-quick time, slamming the book shut and disappearing back to my half-crafted email. In fact, if you tested me on the story I'd just read and I wouldn't have a clue. I wasn't even listening to it! The bedtime story was a chore, a tick on my to-do list, a hindrance to my evening.

The solution ... I moved the bedtime story from my to-do list to what I call my *to-be* list. I started to regard reading a bedtime story as a reward at the end of my day. I stopped judging 'success' by how quickly I could get back to my laptop, but how well I read the story. Things changed, overnight. We'd snuggle up, I'd slow down and add all the funny voices, and it went from chore to bliss.

Nothing external had changed, and yet *everything* had shifted. I'd discovered how to find peace in the madness.

Delete, distort and generalise

Scientists have measured the amount of data that enter the brain and found that an average person processes as much as 74 GB of information a day (that is as much as watching 16 movies) and every year it is about 5% more than the previous year.[17] For context, a couple of hundred years ago, 74 GB of information would be what a highly educated

'Please don't send me any more information. I'm already too well informed.'
Ashleigh Brilliant.
Author & cartoonist.

---

17 Bohn, R. and Short, J. (2012). Measuring Consumer Information. *International Journal of Communication,* 6:980–1000.

person consumed in a lifetime, and we're processing it *every day*.[18] This bombardment is coming at us at a rate of 11 million bits of information per second (as shown in the table below), yet the conscious mind is only able to process about 50 bits per second.[19]

Information transmission rates of the senses	
sensory system	bits per second
eyes	10,000,000
skin	1,000,000
ears	100,000
smell	100,000

If we were to actually process every piece of data that hits our senses we would become overloaded, so at a basic biological level, human beings are filters. That's all we do – take information in, process it and make the best sense of it that we can. There's a tremendous amount of compression taking place to sift 11 million bits of information, and pick out the most important 50.

To protect us from going crazy the information passes through three in-built filters: deletion, distortion and generalisation. Let's look at deletions first. A deletion is where our nervous system just ignores any information that it thinks is not relevant. For example, how many Fs are there in the following sentence:

18 Medium.com. How Much Information Does the Human Brain Learn Every Day? https://medium.com/@askwonder/how-much-information-does-the-human-brain-learn-every-day-92deaad459a6#:~:text=Flux%20Capacity.&text=For%20context%2C%20In%20order%20to,GB)%20of%20data%20a%20day.

19 There's some disagreement on exactly how much data is coming at us, but neuroscientists agree on the general principle that it's A LOT! The wider point is that our brains can only attend to a very small amount of the information.

FINISHED FILES ARE THE RESULT OF YEARS OF SCIENTIFIC STUDY COMBINED WITH THE EXPERIENCE OF MANY YEARS OF EXPERTS.[20]

Deletion takes away much of the superfluous information that bombards our senses. However, and this is the profound bit, the human operating system has an inbuilt negativity bias, which means we might be deleting all the positive information.

You are hardwired to notice bad stuff. It's lovely when someone smiles at you but if someone grimaces and snarls at you, you take serious notice of them because it's dangerous. One bad driver ruins your day – your brain deletes all the good ones. One angry customer upsets you for a week – your brain blanks all the grateful ones. You've got a cancel culture going on between your ears!

Try this general knowledge question for size: *How many animals of each species did Moses take on the ark?*

A fairly simple question, but about 50% of people get it wrong.[21] That's because your brain is applying the second filter, *distortion*. You hear half a story and jump to conclusions, your mind automatically filling in the gaps to make sense of it. It's all done in your subconscious so you're not aware that you're doing it.

---

20 Most people will count three, there are in fact seven.

21 The answer is 'none'. Moses didn't take any animals onto the ark because he was parting the Red Sea at the time. It was his pal Noah that led them in two by two.

While we're on animals, look at the picture and put your hand up when you've spotted the hidden giraffe (NOT the huge giraffe in the middle, the other one!)[22]

As with deletion and distortion, we learn to generalise because it helps us process the world. Generalisation aids us in learning. Once we have learned or experienced something we tend to generalise that that is how it is.

Generalisation is incredibly useful. If we didn't generalise, everything would be new to us all the time. For example, if we didn't generalise that cars were driven the same way, every time we got into a different car we would have to learn to drive all over again. If you have ever driven a strange car with the indicators and windscreen wipers on different control stalks, it takes a while to get used to. You indicate to turn a corner and your windscreen gets another cleaning – until the generalisation is broken (you then get back into your own car and have to reverse the generalisation again!).

22 The word 'giraffe' is written on its neck, which is fairly obvious *after* it has been pointed out.

Can you find the the MISTAKE?

1234567890

So, our brains automatically delete, distort and generalise the world around us so we can make sense of it. These are our filters. Think of it like panning for gold. The only problem is that humans have an inherent bias towards negativity, which means we're accidentally filtering out the nuggets and collecting the gravel!

You can't stop your brain from deleting, distorting and generalising, but you can be aware that you're doing it. Awareness gives you a better chance of panning for gold rather than gravel.

It's about learning to search out new experiences and fresh ways of viewing the world. Often, it's just a matter of refocusing your attention towards the everyday moments of magic. Same world, fresh senses.

For example, go on a favourite walk and notice at least 10 things you have never noticed before. Trust me there will be hundreds. Take pleasure in noticing them. Some might call it mindfulness or being in the moment. The Japanese call it Shinrin Yoku – a walk with your senses switched to 'wide-open' mode. For me, it's the 'beautiful ordinary' and it's everywhere.

Solvitur ambulando [Latin]:

It is solved by walking.

Days to celebrate

Speaking of awareness, have you noticed that every day is some sort of celebration day?

Mother's Day, Father's Day, Remembrance Sunday, World Book Day. Love 'em. But then other days started creeping in. Again, all good …

Disability Awareness, Mental Health Awareness, World Happiness, Pride … which isn't a day, it's a month of partying. I see what you did there.

Then it started to get silly.

Foods jumped on the celebratory band wagon … cheese day, Yorkshire pudding day, national biscuit day, guacamole, ice cream, kale, tripe – they all have their own special days.

Cycle-to-work day, poetry, octopuses, lipstick, bees, turtles, picnics … basically, every single day is now a day to celebrate or remember something.

So, we're adding one more to the calendar. We're Trademarking it as '*Awareness Day* awareness day'™, a reminder that every day is amazing.

All you need is *awareness!*

Every single day is worth celebrating for no other reason than you've woken up. Okay, life might not be perfect, but you're alive – on a planet that has breathable air (at least, for the time being) wi-fi, chocolate brownies and great music.

Mothers, fathers, octopuses, Yorkshire puddings, guacamole, picnics ... we're with you. We'll raise a glass to you on 6th May (for the record, that's Sauvignon Blanc day)

Days to celebrate:

great day	great day	great day	great day
great day	great day	great day	great day
great day	great day	great day	great day
great day	great day	great day	great day

But you're all gatecrashing the biggest celebration of all, the mere fact of the awareness of being alive.

An okay and NOT okay list

This activity works for families and work teams, but also as a useful way of signing up for a pact with yourself.

Write your okay and NOT okay lists. For example, it's okay to have a bad day, it's okay to have a superb day, it's okay to ask for help, it's okay to shine, it's okay to occasionally lose my shit ...

It's NOT okay to doom scroll, it's NOT okay to take my loved ones for granted, it's NOT okay to post angry comments, it's NOT okay to let myself burn out ...

✔ Okay:

_____

_____

_____

_____

NOT okay:

_____

_____

_____

_____ ✗

Agony Uncles

And, finally in this chapter, in the interests of light-heartedness, let's apply some deletion, distortion and generalisation and imagine that Agony Aunts were replaced by Agony Uncles …

Dear Agony Uncle
I hope you can help me. The other day, I left for work, leaving my husband in the house watching TV. My car spluttered, then stalled and broke down about a mile down the road, so I walked back to get my husband's help. When I got home I found him canoodling on the couch with our neighbour's 18-year-old daughter. I confronted him and he said it was a one-off, but I'm not sure I believe him. We've been married for 10 years and have two small children. I love my husband but he's betrayed my trust and I'm at my wits end. I've started drinking wine every single night and I'm struggling to sleep. Even worse, our youngest daughter is picking up the negative vibes and has started wetting the bed.
Please help!
Amelia x

Dear Amelia
A car kangarooing and then stalling after a short distance can be caused by a variety of mechanical faults. Start by checking there is no debris in the fuel line. If it's clear, check the vacuum pipes and hoses on the intake manifold and also check all grounding wires. If none of these approaches solves the problem, I'd suggest it might be a faulty fuel pump causing low delivery pressure to the injectors.
I hope this helps.
Agony Uncle x

#ArtOfBrillBook #Spuddle #ToBeList #HiddenGiraffe #ShinrinYoku
#AwarenessDay #AgonyUncle

EIGHT:
Kindness is a super-power

100% fresh content, crafted around my homemade, soon-to-be world famous Hierarchy of Human Deeds. There's some dubious advice about wearing your swimming cozzie in the winter and being kind to the unkind, but EIGHT has its heart in the right place.

The hierarchy is beautifully book-ended by superheroes. Plot spoiler - if you're interested in swelling the ranks of the Everyday Supers, you'll be needing some special undies.

Confused? Good! Read on ...

'Kindness.
Costs nothing.
Means everything.'

Everyday Supers
Is it a bird? Is it a plane?

… nope, it's an Everyday Superhero.

They're everywhere, but chances are you've never seen an Everyday Super because they're cunningly disguised as ordinary people.

Your mum is an Everyday Super. She probably can't lift cars, *but she can lift you!*

Dads – they might not be able to stop time but they can create time. The most precious time of all. The one-to-one, eye contact, genuinely *being in the moment with their family time.*
Next door neighbours might not have x-ray vision but they can see when you need a hand. Their everyday super-powers are revealed by lending you their ladder.

And have you ever wondered why your besties are your besties? They have the power of empathy. They tune in. They understand. It's a wavelength thing. They are your cheerleaders (no pom-poms required).

All these Everyday Supers have one thing in common – a super-power of ironic proportions! Because, if you stop and think about it, while we all quite fancy the Marvel/DC superhero power of invisibility, it turns out that your Everyday Supers have the total opposite – the power of *visibility.*

In a world of distraction, where everyone is glued to a screen and there's a cat video buffering, ready to snaffle your attention – the power of simply *being there* for someone is quite a thing.

The super-power of presence is your gift to the world so why not join the ranks of the Everyday Supers. Embrace your viz-ability and availability.

The Hierarchy of Human Kind

'We do have a lot in common. The same earth, the same air, the same sky. Maybe if we started to look at what's the same instead of what's different ... well, who knows?'

Meowth. Pokémon.

'Self-help' is all well and good but why is there no bookshop section on 'helping others'? If there was, this chapter would be its centrepiece.

The vast majority of people are absolutely lovely. Stupidly busy, rushing around, eyes locked on their phone ... but lovely.

Some are a bit less nice. They might be stuck in some sort of life situation that has sucked the loveliness out of them but you know their prickliness is temporary. The milk of human kindness is in there, but right at this moment, it's a bit semi-skimmed. Hey, we've all been there.

I noticed that Abe Maslow made a name for himself with his fabled Hierarchy of Needs so I've gone one better and created my very own brand spankingly new Hierarchy of *Deeds*.

Maslow's was a pyramid of self-actualisation but mine's much simpler, it's a pyramid of human kind. Follow it to the top and you'll be squeezing a pale of full-fat kindness from the udder of life.

Here's the rascal.

The Hierarchy of Human Kind

7 — Human Kind

6 — Be Kind to the unKind

5 — RAK 'em up — Anonymously

4 — RAK 'em up

Niceness Ninja

3 — Kindness for no reason

2 — Be Kind to your future self RIGHT NOW

Bucket filler

1 — Be Kind to yourself

Let me explain. The bottom three levels are about filling your own kindness bucket. Four, five and six are about kindness 'leakage' and level seven is modern day superhero status.

Warning, each level comes with a challenge.

Strap yourself in and let's build up from ground zero ...

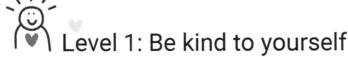

Level 1: Be kind to yourself

Yes, kindness starts with you being nice to you. It seems like an obvious place to start but, funnily enough, this is the level that people struggle with the most!

We all have an inner critic, a nagging voice of self-doubt that provides a running commentary about how rubbish we are. It works in the opposite way to the judiciary system – in the court of self-judgment, you're presumed guilty every time!

Psychologists call it negativity bias. Professor Steve Peters calls it your inner chimp.[23] I've also developed a technical term for it. I call it 'being human'.

This inner critic is built into the human operating system and every cell in your body is eavesdropping on your inner dialogue. Hence why the bottom level of the Human Kindness pyramid starts very close to home – *inside your own head!*

Catch yourself doing things well, give yourself a bit of encouragement, compliment yourself on a situation well handled. I'm advising that you do this quietly, in your thoughts, because

23 Prof. Steve Peters. *The Chimp Paradox*. Vermillion Life Essentials, 2020

an out loud, 'Oh my goodness, did you all notice how I had the confidence to speak up in the meeting just now. Am I epic, or what?' can sound a bit narcissistic.

It just so happens that the modern world deals you loads of situations to beat yourself up about, from mild to acute. To calm the civil war between your ears, have a go at the activity below.

The power of 'I AM ...'

Your ego is your identity. It's who you think you are. All too often we talk down to ourselves with a negative running commentary; I'm not confident, I'm not as smart my co-workers, I'm not as good looking as so-and-so, I'm rubbish with numbers.

Once you assume that identity, you become that person!

To upgrade to a better version of you, you need to change your 'I AM' statements to something more inspiring.

I AM confident
I AM a good learner
I AM beautiful
I AM capable of becoming good with numbers

Basically, whatever follows 'I AM' will come looking for you.

This is too powerful to be left hanging so I'm leaving space for you to write your own 10 positive I AM statements.

1. I am loving
2.
3.
4.
5.
6.
7.
8.
9.
10.

Remember, you become what you believe so whatever follows 'I AM' will seek you out. 'I AM' will chase you down. It will catch up with you and you will become 'I AM ...'

So it makes sense to upgrade your I AMs.

Level 2: Be kind to your future self
RIGHT NOW

This level is about self-care and, in particular, making choices that your future self will thank you for. That sentence needs a bit of unpicking …

'Self-care' basically says that you can't pour from an empty cup. You cannot give what you haven't got. Applying it to you, you can't give your family love, positivity and confidence unless you first possess those qualities. It boils down to this; the best thing you will ever do for the people you love is take really good care of yourself.

Yes, I know, that sounds selfish but it's actually the least selfish thing you will ever do. The people you share your life with need you fizzing with energy, enthusiasm and positivity.

That means you have to make good choices about your inner voice (less negativity in your head, less beating yourself up about how rubbish you are) and, crucially, you have to make good attitudinal choices.

Taking it to into the future is where self-care gets immensely powerful. I've become better at looking after myself now (in this moment) while also keeping a lookout for the wellbeing of my *future* self. So, basically, I've got an eye on my wellbeing tomorrow, next week, next month and next year.

Yes, it's a bit spooky, but *today's* me is looking out for the *future* me.

For example, you've had a tough day at work so you might seek some self-care in a glass of wine. The first glass feels good, your stress is ebbing away so it makes sense to have another glass and before you know it there's an empty bottle. That might feel good right now but it's not being kind to tomorrow's self; the you who is groggy, sleep deprived and hazy all day.

Note, this is a stunningly simple concept that I overlooked for years. Being kind to yourself now whilst keeping an eye on the wellbeing of the future you is a much bigger deal than it sounds on paper.

Before I knew any of this 'future self' stuff I was really good at making bad choices. For example, someone opened a packet of biscuits and that was it. Biscuits need eating and I was a good eater, so I'd would down the entire packet.

A celeb who also makes bad choices:

'Fruit ... or Cookie ... Fruit ... Cookie ... Me, Cookie Monster! This No-Brainer!'

Cookie Monster, Sesame Street.

But not anymore. Eating several packets of biscuits a week isn't good for my waistline, or my diabetes in two years' time. So, yes, I might snaffle a biscuit or two but the packet goes back into the tin because I'm looking after my *future* self.

Hey, I don't want to bore you with my examples, I want you to come up with some of your own, but here's another biggy. The old version of me (i.e., the normal version of me before I learned all this stuff) would always find an excuse not to get fit. I'd make the decision to go for a run but the sky was looking a bit grey and that was enough for me to make an excuse; I can't go for a jog in case it rains.

Now I'm looking after my future self it makes perfect sense to go for a run, whatever the weather, because I'll be fit, healthy and buzzing with life. That's good for me, and my family.

I suggest you change your outlook and have a right good go at looking after yourself now (in this moment) while also keeping an eye on the wellbeing of your future self. You'll find things that used to be difficult – eating healthy food, getting good sleep, looking after your fitness, drinking less alcohol – all of a sudden become a whole lot easier. There's a future version of you that will thank you for the choices you're making today.

Level 2 of the pyramid hints at this: don't let your future self down!

Level 3: Kindness for no reason

Remember, levels 1, 2 and 3 are about you filling your own happiness bucket, so here are some deliriously weird top kindness tips that will help you engage with the gift of life, inspired by my writing buddy, Mr Will Hussey.[24]

Hug your dog, sisters, brothers, cat, goldfish and parents; not necessarily in that order, or at the same time. If all else fails, just try to live up to being the person your dog thinks you are. #BeMoreDog

Listen to your favourite music. Make music. Go to watch people perform music. Sing if you can and most definitely sing if you can't. Sing like you're in the shower.

Go outside every day, whatever the weather. Celebrate the storms, bathe in the sunlight, dance in the moonlight. Howl at the moon.

---

24 I've co-authored several books with Will, including *Zest: How to Squeeze the Max Out of Life*. Check Will out here: https://www.willhussey.co.uk/

Look up at the stars. Often! Wear your wellies in the summer and your swimming cozzie in the winter.

Camp out in your back garden. Pick a nice summer's evening, no tent necessary. Sleep under the stars. Watch the universe shine. You are made of that! (Note, if it's raining, camping in your lounge is acceptable.)

Interact with people. Virtual ones are okay but real people are better, preferably the ones who make you smile.

Go to bed a bit earlier and sleep well. It actually cleans your brain. Yes, really!

Picnics are a heady combo of food, people and outdoors. Most people don't have enough picnics in their life. Don't be most people!

Advice for the modern world
'Dance like nobody's watching. Email like it might be read out at a tribunal.'

See everything with a fresh pair of eyes. When you wake up, imagine it's your first day. Be wide eyed and amazed. Greet your family as though you've been away for six years. Look at a tree and imagine it's the first time you've ever seen a tree. Hug it if you want to. *Be amazed!*

Be a good friend to yourself. You know that good advice you give to your best friend? Don't worry about it; it doesn't matter, don't take it personally, it was only an interview, he's not worth it anyway … take that advice!

Oh, and remember, you're never too old to learn something stupid!

Level 4: RAKs (Random Acts of Kindness)

When you've got your own kindness bucket full to the brim you'll know because it starts overflowing. Welcome to level 4!

> I am not impressed by your money, position or title. I am impressed by how you treat others.

Science (and common sense) tells us that the quickest way to feel amazing is to do a good deed for someone else. Random acts of kindness can range from a smile, a chat, holding a door open, making someone a cuppa, telling someone they're ace, giving a hug, cleaning up a mess, holding a hand, paying a compliment, etc. The point being, they're totally random. You didn't plan them. There was an opportunity for kindness and you took it.

Here's one from earlier today; I was in the supermarket queue for the self-service till. I had about 20 items in my basket and the woman behind me had two. So I let her nip in front of me. It made her day, and mine!

Simple, spur of the moment, free … and we both had better days because of it. So go ahead punk, make someone's day.

Level 5: *Anonymous* RAKs

These are some acts of kindness that you never get recognised for. You do them with stealth, like a ninja. You spot an opportunity, do your act of kindness, and leave. Nobody knows it was you and therefore you get no thanks.

Let me give you an example. I was driving across a toll bridge and I paid twice; once for my car and also for the car behind me. I had no idea who was in that car but I'm hoping that being waived through for free will have put a smile on their face.

Whether it did or not, doesn't really matter. What matters is that anonymous random act of kindness put a huge grin on *my* face! I enjoyed doing it and, bizarrely, it was even more enjoyable because the other driver will never know it was me. It happened years ago and is still making me happy today!

Look, you might already be doing these wonderful deeds. If not, have a go. I guarantee you'll feel amazing.

Level 6: Be kind to the unkind

'When they go low, we go high.'

Michelle Obama. Former first lady, now author and TV host.

Brace yourself, in fact you might need to sit down before absorbing this one. It's super-advanced, high-level, nosebleed, kindness territory.

No matter how fabulous you are, there will always be unkind people.

I'm guessing that when kindness was being handed out, some people were at the back of the queue and there was none left. The modern world has made it easier than ever to be unkind. In the olden days haters might have whispered behind your back or had a grumble in their head, but now they can tap away at a keyboard and spit negativity at anyone and everyone.

'Social media made folks way too comfortable with disrespecting people and not getting punched in the face for it.'

Mike Tyson. Former heavyweight boxing champion.

It's worth mentioning that it's usually hurt people who hurt people. The trolls will always be there. My attack dog tagline is this: if you can't beat 'em, definitely don't join 'em.

My level 6 challenge to you is this; if you're going to earn the kindness black belt, you have to be super-kind to everyone. Yes, even the one or two unkind people who don't seem to deserve it. If they're not very nice people that's because they've not experienced enough kindness or love.

So to reach the top of the Pyramid of Human Kind you have to love the unloved, be nice to the not-so-nice and be kind to the unkind.

That gets you to level 7, the peak of kindness, a fully paid-up member of 'human kind'. I'm thinking of getting some badges done.

It all points to this: be a go-giver as well as a go-getter. In a world that is dominated by differences, let kindness be your religion.

Amen.

Space to reflect on kindness that's been done to you,
that you have done for others, and to scribble your
'human-kindness attack plan'.

Unleash your special undies

This chapter has focused on the super-powers of visibility, availability and kindness. Everyone knows that superheroes wear their underwear on the outside, so if you're going to swell the ranks of the Everyday Supers, you'll be needing some special pants.

So here's a favour you can do for yourself and your partner, right now ...

Pop upstairs to your bedroom and open your underwear drawer. In that drawer there will be some undies that you don't really fancy. If you're unsure which undies I'm talking about, it's the misshapen off-colour ones you wear when you're poorly. Or gardening.

I want you to identify these last-resort knickers and remove them from your drawer. Bin them, burn them or bury them in your garden so you never have to wear them again.Because tomorrow, when you're showered, deodorised and getting dressed, you will open your underwear drawer and in there will be your 'special pants'. Once again, you know *exactly* which ones I mean.

And I want you to wear your special underwear for work tomorrow. That means when you pull up in the car park and stroll in to work you will have a certain sparkle, a swagger and *je ne sais quoi* because you know what's cracking off down below.

Please note, my special pants top tip is not just a giggle. Positive psychology has a term – *enclothed cognition* – which means super-duper underwear is a legit way of making you feel good.

The sad fact is that on Monday morning most people's aim is to get through the week or survive until their next holiday. Humanity is in the collective habit of wishing our weeks away and placing happiness as a dot on the horizon.

Similarly, we tend to save our 'special pants' for a special occasion.

Rewind back to a fact from earlier in the book: the average lifespan is 4000 weeks. Life is indeed a very short and precious gift. You've got 4000 weeks to make a dent in the universe so my 'special pants' top tip is simply a wake-up call. It's a reminder to quit waiting.

Every day is a special pants day because LIFE is the ultimate special occasion.

Every day is a Special PANTS day

Life's too short. QUIT waiting for happiness

#ArtOfBrillBook #SuperYOU #EverydaySupers #HierarchyOfDeeds
#Kindness #IAm #SpecialPants

NINE: Your F**ckit List

A swear word (albeit a blanked out one), in the chapter title! That's madness. It'll attract 1-star reviews! I'll risk it on the grounds that people who hate the book will have given up way earlier than this, their single stars shining brightly in the Amazon sky.

I'm over it.

One of the strongest chapters in the book, NINE explores comfort zones and belief systems via a circus elephant, before getting to the offending word. There's a whale of a tale, a permission slip and bucket loads of cracking content.

But first things first, we start with some wisdom from the mouths of babes.

Here are a few nuggets of wisdom about LOVE and LIFE, from the mouths of babes ...

'You gotta say your affirmations in your mouth and your heart. You say, "I am brave of this meeting!", "I am loved", "I smell good!"'

Isaak, age 6

'Never put a skunk on a bus.'

Milo, age 5

'Think about the donuts of your day! Even if you cry a little, you can think about potato chips!'

Tommy, age 7

'Even if it's a yucky day, you can get a hug.'

Femi, age 4

'You gotta take a deep breath and you gotta do it again.'

Abi, age 8

'When someone loves you, the way they say your name is different. You just know that your name is safe in their mouth.'

Billy, age 4

'When your mom is mad at your dad, don't let her brush your hair.'

Taylia, age 11

'Love is when you go out to eat and give somebody most of your French fries without making them give you any of theirs.'

Chrissie, age 6

'Kindness is what makes you smile when you're tired.'

Terri, age 4

'Monsters are less scary when they're peeing.'

Tommy, age 6

'Happiness is when your puppy licks your face even after you left him alone all day.'

Mary Ann, age 4

Rage against the mundane

The diagram below represents a relatively simple way of illustrating some of the key themes of this book.

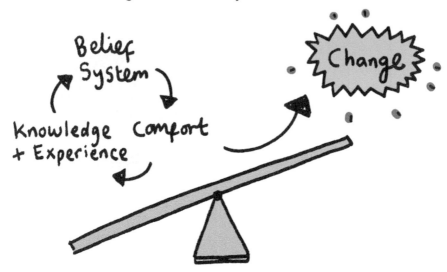

Your brain's primary purpose is to keep you safe, which is why it loves familiarity, habits, repetitive behaviours and routines. So, for example, the alarm goes off at the same time every morning and your routine kicks in. If you've got a family, there's an order in which people go into the bathroom. You've got a seat allocated at the kitchen table, which is where you perch as you eat the same breakfast, slurping the same tea/coffee (black/white ... it'll be what you always have), probably from your favourite mug. You might even have a different favourite mug for tea and coffee.

You get the picture. It's the same commute, listening to the same radio station or podcasts. If you're commuting to your upstairs office you'll sit down and log onto whatever websites you usually check before you start work.

At surface level, there's nothing wrong with these routines. They make us feel safe. But the habits can also become ingrained in our thinking, which is where they can become our downfall. Our comfort zones can restrict us. It's estimated that each of us has about 80,000 thoughts a day, of which the vast majority are exactly the same thoughts as yesterday!

Same thinking, same results is a safety mechanism. You survived yesterday so your brain puts a big tick in the 'safety' box. It's achieved its number one priority of keeping you in the game so it makes sense to do exactly the same again tomorrow.

And the next day. And the next day ...

The result? We forget to stretch, and life can become very samey.

> Spice up your life with this advice ...
> I'm the kind of person who stops the microwave at 1 second just to feel like a bomb diffuser.

Skipping back to the earlier diagram, your comfort zones arise from your knowledge and experience that, in turn, is determined by your belief system. This is a biggy. Our belief system is a deep-rooted view of the world that manifests itself in the way we speak, think and behave.

Beliefs can be very deeply rooted. *People die for them!*

If you want genuine, long-lasting change, some of your beliefs need to be uprooted. With that in mind, here's a story about an elephant that isn't really about an elephant at all ...

There was an elephant who travelled with a circus. 'Nellie' is too obvious, so let's go with … Mrs Philomena Shardlow.

The owner figured that the elephant was one of the main attractions so he always positioned Mrs Philomena Shardlow at the entrance to the big top. All the children had the thrill of lining up and feeding the elephant on the way in. Except, of course, you can't just let an elephant loose. Mrs Shardlow has to be tethered. So, if you looked closely, you'd see that the four-ton beast had a rope around her left back ankle. If you looked even closer you'd notice the rope was tied to a tent peg, and the tent peg was hammered into the grass.

Let me revise the scenario. You have a four-ton beast with a rope around its ankle, tied to a tent peg. It's been raining so the tent peg isn't hammered into the ground. The elephant keeper has just pushed the tent peg into the soft turf with the palm of his hand. 'There, that should hold you.'

Why doesn't Mrs S do a runner? Why doesn't she take a look at the flimsy and inadequate tether and disappear to Greggs to get some sticky buns?

The answer is, of course, that Mrs Shardlow's comfortable. She's being fed and watered. Mrs S has got a routine and besides, she doesn't think she can escape because when she was a calf she had a chain wrapped around her ankle, and the chain was padlocked to a lamp post. No matter how hard she tried to escape, it just resulted in a sore ankle.

Now Mrs Shardlow's grown up, she's learned that she can't escape. Her knowledge and experience is that she tried to escape but couldn't.

So, what's really holding the elephant back? The rope? The keeper? The fact that she's getting fed every night?

No. Mrs Philomena Shardlow's *belief* system is what's stopping her. The rope is a symbol. She's an example of what psychologists call 'learned helplessness'. Please excuse the clumsiness of the next sentence – it's hard to write without sounding rude, but …

… are you Mrs Philomena Shardlow?

Is there something in your belief system that's holding you back?

You don't change behaviour at the level of behaviour. For real breakthroughs, you need to change your belief systems.

To help you change you need to understand that humans are learning machines. We're built to acquire knowledge and skills. But we're really bad at un-learning! I'm talking *seriously* bad! Once you've got something in your head, it can be quite difficult to get it out again.

Not impossible, but difficult. To raise your personal bar to 'best self' requires a balance of taking on some new knowledge whilst also letting go of old habits that aren't serving you well. This will be difficult until it becomes your default.

Your F*ckit List

Most people are familiar with a bucket list of things that want to achieve before they die. These tend to be long held ambitions – BIG things that are outside your comfort zone. Too many people die with these things unticked because there's a chasm of difference between *wishing* for them and *making* them happen.

Recently, I met a conference delegate who described himself as 'emotionally constipated', which he clarified thus: 'I haven't given a shit in months.'

To be clear, I want you to care. *Wholeheartedly!* But to protect your sanity you need to care about the *right* things and let the other stuff fall away.

To break out of your comfort zone you need to write a f*ckit list. This is a list of things you're going to have to STOP doing in order to achieve your bucket ambitions. You need some steely determination when writing your f*ckit list. What thoughts, ideas, routines, habits and beliefs are you willing to give up to improve your life?

I've made some personal changes. For example, unnecessary meetings and, in particular, meetings *about* meetings – they're difficult to erase, but have been massively reduced.

Drinking rubbish coffee, staying in cheap hotels, watching trashy TV, eating bad food ... I've binned them. Life's too short.

Pay attention to when you're scrolling and scrolling and scrolling ... do you feel alive, connected and joyful? If so, scroll on. If not, stick 'endlessly scrolling' on your f*ckit list.

To get good at being you, there are lots of things you can learn to do but, equally, it's about *unlearning* the behaviours and habits of thinking that are sabotaging your awesomeness. Thus, your bucket and f*ckit lists go hand in hand.

These two questions will focus your attention on what you need to STOP doing:

Which *behaviours* are you willing to give up in order to achieve what you want? (example: less doom scrolling, cut out some TV, low-level grumbling, procrastinating, playing small ...)

Which *habits of thinking* are you willing to give up in order to achieve what you want? (example: putting yourself down, self-doubt, worrying about what other people think, inner critic ...)

Crystalise the above into these personal commitments:

These are the three things I'm going to start doing (or do more of)	These will be the benefits to me and those around me
1.	
2.	
3.	

These are the three things I'm going to STOP doing (or do less of)	These will be the benefits to me and those around me
1.	
2.	
3.	

The elimination diet:
REMOVE:

regret
guilt
blame
anger
resentment
worry

Then, watch your health and life, improve.

Charles F. Glassman.

The Jonah Complex

We're all delivered into this world in the same way – naked and screaming. (A quick and potentially disturbing thought … if you leave this world in the same way, it's either the apocalypse or a terribly bad day in your care home!)

Someone cuts the umbilical cord, the midwife rubs a flannel over you, wraps you in a towel and hands you to your mum. You look, blurry eyed, at your mum and she smiles down at you. It's love at first sight. There's a bond and, fingers crossed, that's the start of what psychologists call a secure attachment.

Wind yourself back to *that* moment. At one-hour old you are a mass of pure potential. The possibilities are endless. You – one-hour old – it's knee-shakingly exciting to imagine what you could achieve.

Hey, it's not just you. At one-hour old, we *all* have unimaginable potential.

Then we get to, say, age 57 (i.e., me right now!) and we reach the point of wishing we could get a mirror with a better view. What happened to all that potential. All that stuff the man in the mirror *could* have done and all those things I *could* have achieved … why does my reflection look and feel so average?

By way of explanation, let me introduce you to the little-known but deeply profound Jonah Complex.

Backstory, Jonah was the guy in the Quran and Bible who got swallowed by a whale and seeing that the Jonah Complex has a religious origin, I'll start with the parable (as told in my own words, with absolutely no offence intended) and then extrapolate to today.

Picture the scene. We're way back in history, 2700 years ago, in a bustling market somewhere in the Middle East. It's hot, dusty and chaotic. The stalls are set cheek to jowl and there's the usual market place cacophony. Stall holders are calling out their wares, flies are buzzing around the meat, the fruit is rotting in the heat, beggars are a-begging and hagglers a-haggling.

Jonah was part of the swarm. He owned and ran a market stall that let's say, for imaginative purposes, sold footwear. Quite timid by nature, he was one of the quieter ones. Jonah went about his businesses, eking out a living and then, one day, out of the blue, God asked him for a favour. He commanded Jonah to go to the city of Nineveh to deliver a message. It was a big message and Jonah was a timid guy. I'm imagining the conversation must have been along these lines:

God (in a booming voice): 'JONAH, I COMMAND YOU GO TO THE CITY OF NINEVEH AND DELIVER A BIT OF BAD NEWS.'

Jonah (squinting up into the sky, hand to his forehead to shield the burning sun, and looking confused): 'What me, boss? I'm just Jonah who owns "Sandals-R-Us". I'm no messenger. I'm the guy who sells flip-flops. You must mean another Jonah. One with a bit more about him. There are quite a few Jonahs on the market, do you want me to ask around? Thanks for thinking of me, but I'd rather not go to Nineveh. It's a heck of a walk.'

I'm guessing. I wasn't actually there.

The long and short of it is that, quite famously, Jonah declined God's request and got swallowed by a whale for his troubles.

Lurking in the parable is the fact that Jonah preferred to play small. He shrank back from the challenge, which gives rise to the so-called Jonah Complex ... the reason we don't live up to our potential is not that we can't, but that we *daren't*.

We're running scared of our own greatness!

Although we talk a good talk about 'living our best life' and 'being our best self', we're actually spooked by the reality of it. It might be too daunting to be stand-out amazing. If I come to work with a grin on my face, people will think I'm a weirdo. What if it's too difficult to be my best self, or what if I try to raise my personal bar and fail?

The Jonah Complex says it's safer to play small. It's easier to fit in rather than stand out so we talk ourselves down from the heady heights of being a two-percenter.

I have no idea whether the Jonah Complex holds any water for you personally, but the fear of our own greatness is a point well worth considering because it suggests the biggest thing stopping you from shining is YOU!

If the possibility of being remarkable shoots a thunderbolt of fear into you, here's something to consider. Looping back to the fact that life's a short and precious gift, what's the point of aiming for mediocre? Why would we settle for middle-of-the-pack. Why would you set an average bar for being a parent, spouse or employee?

You're much better than that!

SHINE
is my
favourite
Colour

Marc Jacobs. Fashion designer.

Here are two massive points:

The Jonah Complex says that all eight billion of us have amazingness factory-fitted into our human operating system, but we opt to keep it hidden.

It's like owning a Ferrari and driving it at 26 mph. I mean, what's the point?

Maybe it's time to show up in life as your best self?

But there's a bigger thought lurking. Abe Maslow spoke of what he called 'eupsychia', the culture created by thousands of people who are all being their best selves.

That's what the world needs, and while you can't command anyone else, you can lead by example.

To help you get over the Jonah Complex I've written you a permission slip. It's your ticket to SHINE.

Your permission slip is valid for the rest of your life and you can use it as often as you want.

All you have to do is sign it and remember to use it when you need it.

Time to get your SHINE on! → → →

Permission Slip

I, [please print your name here]

hereby give myself permission to be the two-percenter version of me. I will not be embarrassed to be STAND-OUT AMAZING. Instead, I will SHINE and let others catch the glow.

From this day forward, I'm granting myself permission to change what needs changing. I empower myself to love and be loved. I will pat myself on the back when I've earned it, forgive myself when I mess up and allow myself to ask for help when I need it. I have my consent to let go of negative thinking and habits that might be holding me back.

I don't need anyone else's approval, I need mine. Therefore, I am handing responsibility for my future to me. I am in agreement with myself to raise my personal bar, go for my dreams and to give life a right good go.

I acknowledge that life will not roll out the red carpet for me. I am in charge of the choices I make and the effort required. I am granting myself permission to get excited about doing the heavy lifting that will be needed to craft the life that I want.

The 'I am not enough' mantra is actually true. The fact is that I'm waaaaaay more than enough. I'm a one-in-eight-billion miracle. That's why I'm in agreement with myself to quit playing small. No more waiting. No more Jonah Complex! Starting now, I have the personal stamp of approval to BE myself and to LIKE myself. Not on an over-the-top sickly self-love way, but in a quietly confident 'I've got this' way.

It might not be easy, but it'll be worth it. Best self and best life, I'm coming at ya!

Ashes to ashes.
Dust to dust.
Funk to funky.
Till death do I part.
BECAUSE I'M WORTH IT

LOVE,
Me [Please sign your name here]

.... Date ....

#ArtOfBrillBook #F*ckitList #MrsShardlow #JonahComplex #Eupsychia
#PermissionSlip

NEVER assume that LOUD is STRONG or quiet is weak, it's often the other way around.

TEN: The 90/10 Principle

Must have more!!

The world's a bit moreish. We want more, chase more, do more, consume more, eat more, drink more and lust for more. We're the first humans in the history of the planet to be dying from over-consumption.

TEN invites you to join the rebels who commit to having less and doing less, but *being* more. That requires an attitudinal shift and a slap on your wrists every time you waste time and energy trying to control the uncontrollables. The chapter delivers some bombshell news about the days of the week. Plot spoiler – you thought there were seven, there is only one. It's always choose-day.

Before you start, here's a thought experiment. Imagine if the *Titanic* had set sail from Southampton and arrived safely in New York. In which case, there would be no such thing as Leo Decaprio, Kate Winslett or crinkum-crankum.

Confused? *You will be!*

Calling all the rebels ...

I'm kicking this chapter off with a big thought. Please note, this is not a political point, just an innocent observation.

Communities and societies develop based on knowledge that seems right at the time, which is why pretty much forever, we've been chasing economic growth. On one level, it makes perfect sense. If you genuinely think that having more stuff will make you happy, you create an economy that facilitates having more stuff.

So that's what we've been doing. Individually and collectively, we've ploughed headlong into materialism. We built the economy on a bedrock of offering citizens more choice, more products, more comfort ... governments were elected on their promises to make the economy grow, which would make us richer, because that's genuinely what we thought was the right thing to do.

Stuffocation (definition):
The feeling of being overwhelmed by the stuff that one has bought or accumulated.

Leads to stuffocating (definition):
drowning in glut.

If we fast forward from, say 50 or 100 years ago, to NOW, and we look around at our communities, both local and global, we might be regretting our drive for economic growth.

Mother Earth is struggling. Our drive for materialism means she's running out of rainforests, clean water, polar icecaps and breathable air. In an effort to give us what we thought we wanted, the old girl is wheezing a bit.

So, yes, we've got more stuff and more choice but if we compare our levels of happiness – now versus 70 years ago – you'll find we're much richer but not a single percentage point happier.[25]

Hey, I'm not suggesting we go back to the bad old days of diphtheria, rickets and outside toilets. Economic growth, on the whole, has been fabulous. That said, we've also got food banks, and rising levels of anxiety, depression and suicide.

It's not just the forests that are burning. Despite all the accoutrements of modernity, human burnout is well ablaze.

What envy feels like...

I'm suggesting that we might have made some poor choices. We've accidentally put 'wealth' above 'relationships'. If we'd kept relationships with real flesh and blood family and friends at the top

25 MentalHealthToday.co.uk. People Were Happier in 1957 than Today. https://www.mentalhealthtoday.co.uk/people-were-happier-in-1957-than-today-according-to-research#:~:text=People%20living%20in%201957%20were,60%20years%20%20according%20to%20research

of our list of priorities, we'd have built communities that might have had less, but *been* more.

But, hey, anyone suggesting we take a backwards economic step is going to have rotten fruit thrown at them, so let me park the 'wealth' idea and leave you with this ...

> 'I can't go back to yesterday – because I was a different person then.'
>
> Alice. Alice in Wonderland.

While we can't turn the clock back, we can set a new starting point, we can pledge to be at the *start* of the wellbeing revolution.

The rebels have already realised that underneath all the conditioning that has convinced us we need to have more, pursue more and do more, the only thing we actually have to do is *be* more. That means less busyness, less mania, less rushing headlong through our days (weeks, months and years), less consumption ...

... and more *being*.

Being with family. *Being* with friends. *Being* in relationships. *Being* kind. *Being* nice.

That means less investment in stuff and a subtle shift towards an investment in those closest to you.

Be a rebel. Raise your own personal bar. Lead the mental WEALTH revolution. Commit to being a human being, instead of a human doing.

Controlling the controllables

Before you get stuck into this section it is worth bearing in mind that the most difficult thing to learn is something you think you know already. Heads up, this is that bit!

Things that Matter

Things you CONTROL

what you should FOCUS on

There are only two things you can truly be in control of:

Your preparation for what *might* happen and your *response* to what has just happened.

The universe is pretty much in control of everything else!

The 90/10 principle preps you for both.

It suggests that 10% of whether you have a good day or a bad day is down to what happens to you. So, for example, your train is cancelled, or you're stuck in a traffic jam, or you're camping in the rain, or you've got back-to-back meetings with no time to actually get anything done!

You can't control the 10% – 'life' happens to you every single day.

The 90/10 principle suggests that 90% of whether you have a good day or bad day is about how to choose to *respond* to the 10%.

So, basically, you can't control the train cancellation, traffic, weather or workload … they're going to happen whether you want them to or not. The remaining 90% of whether you have a good day or bad day is down to your response to these situations.

Your *attitude* is the 90%, and that's massive!

Once you realise you can choose a better attitude, you'll find your day goes a whole lot better. Everyday events become so much easier to handle.

Train cancellation – it's not ideal but the 90/10 principle puts you in control. Instead of stressing, you make a call, send an email and put Plan B into operation.

Camping in the rain – it's not the perfect situation – but rather than sitting in your tent grumbling about it being the worst holiday ever, you put your wellies on and go jumping in the puddles.
In the examples above, the exact the same things are happening to you, but a different choice of attitude gets you a much better outcome.

The 90/10 principle boils down to this: that person in the bathroom mirror has a lot more control over your day than you think.

My research into the two-percenters points to a collective set of habits, of which one stands out as more important than the rest. It's going to seem obvious when you read it but as I explain in my training, it's common sense, but not common practice.

Are you ready?

The number one thing that two-percenters do that the rest of the population doesn't do, is ...
... *choose to be positive!*

Told you it'd seem obvious but I'm going to say it again so it sinks into your bone marrow. All the upbeat, extraordinary people in my PhD surveys have all made a conscious decision to craft an attitude that works in their favour.[26]

There's some effort involved in choosing a positive attitude but once you know how, it becomes what I call a 'portable benefit'. That means your attitude travels with you. It comes to work with you, it attends meetings with you, it comes home with you ...
because it IS you.

---

26 Social science is riddled with imperfections and I am by no means claiming to be a stats geek. But for those who crave academic rigour, in order to limit the probability of Type 1 errors, I applied the Bonferroni correction. This adjusted the p-value to a more stringent 0.029 (a-value /number of tests which is, in this case, 0.05/17). Post hoc comparisons using t-test with Bonferroni correction revealed significant results for, '*I choose to be positive*' ($t(78) = 8.38$, $p < 0.001$).

Nuanced but important ...

The idea of happiness has been hijacked in recent years. It's been weaponised against us. Social media tells you to choose to be happy. We're given the impression that happiness is the norm and anything outside joy is a problem to be solved or medicated.

As someone who's been studying human flourishing for two decades, I promise you humans are not built for permanent happiness. We're designed to respond to external stimuli and those are constantly changing. Emotions are like weather patterns, they blow over. So, basically, you can live a happy life and not be happy all of the time. The trick is to live the full range of emotions, including the black clouds and hurricanes.

You can, however, learn to live in a happier climate.

As for choosing to be happy, quite frankly, don't believe the hype. Happiness is an emotion. You can open up to it and allow more in, but you can't choose it.

Positivity on the other hand ... is not an emotion. It's an attitude, and is therefore something that you can learn to take charge of.

Bottom line, from the doctor of happiness, if you can craft a great attitude, happiness is not guaranteed, but more likely.

Groundhog Day

To be clear, choosing to have a positive attitude doesn't make problems disappear. It doesn't stop the rain, it doesn't make climate change go away, it doesn't make your football team win. A great attitude doesn't make your train turn up on time and no matter how positive you choose to be, adversity and unfairness will still exist.

What a positive attitude will do is to put you in a better position to deal with the rain, climate emergency, your team losing and your train being cancelled. Instead of stopping you in your tracks, these glitches are obstacles to be overcome. While everyone else is negative about the world, you live in a world of possibilities and your positivity shines through.

Choosing to carry an attitude that works *in your favour* is a massive power-up.

Who taught you this?

Monday   Tuesday   Wednesday   Thursday   Friday

Basically, whatever day of the week your calendar says it is, it's always *choose*-day!

Here are some positive choices that you can start making, right now:

Choose progress over perfection.

Choose courage over fear.

Choose responding positively over reacting negatively.

Choose losing and learning over winning and celebrating.

Choose optimism over pessimism.

Choose you over trying to be someone else.

Choose acceptance over judgement.

Choose hard work over an easy life.

Choose doing what's right over doing what's easiest.

Choose botheredness over can't-be-botheredness.

Choose kindness over meanness.

Choose Mondays over Fridays.

Choose giving it a go over giving up.

Choose personal responsibility over blaming others.

Choose opening your eyes rather than rolling your eyes.

But most of all, choose what this chapter's been all about.

The attitude you carry around with you will affect your entire day so it pays to choose positive over negative.

It matters!
It *really* matters!

'It's our choices, Harry, that show what we truly are, far more than our abilities.'

Albus Dumbledore.
End-of-level Wizard boss.

Have a go at the following activity. If it hasn't already, the penny will surely drop ...

How would the mood hoover and two-percenter version of you act in the following situations:

A work colleague needs your help when you're busy.

mood hoover _____

_____

2%er _____

_____

You make a mistake.

mood hoover _____

_____

2%er _____

_____

You disagree with someone.

mood hoover _____

_____

2%er _____

_____

Somebody cuts you up at the traffic lights.

mood hoover

2%er

There's a 20-minute queue at the supermarket.

mood hoover

2%er

Your grumpy relatives are coming to stay for a week.

mood hoover

2%er

You're camping and it's pouring with rain.

mood hoover

2%er

If you've thought this through properly, you'll notice you feel and behave much more positively as a two-percenter, and that the outcome will be different in each scenario.

The 90/10 principle is very simple yet very few people actually apply it to their lives. All the instances in the previous exercise are 90/10 scenarios. Camping in the rain, queuing, being cut up in the traffic – these are the 10%. We cannot control the event but we're absolutely in charge of how we *choose* to react. This is the 90%.

Once you understand the 90/10 rule, you can begin to wrestle back some control of your reactions, and better reactions trigger more favourable outcomes.

Crinkum-crankum

Crinkum-crankum is one of those words that you have to say out loud. Go ahead, give it a go. Turn to the person sitting next to you and let the words out of your mouth, slowly and clearly:

Crinkum. Crankum.

Crinkum-crankum describes something that's full of twists and turns. Rollercoasters, cheese strings and life are all *crinkum-crankum*.

Let me guess – if your life was a movie, it'd have a superb cast but you're struggling to figure out the plot. So my advice is to change your story. When things don't turn out as you expected, instead of *'disaster'*, *'problem'* or *'nightmare'* I'd like you to start shouting out, *'Crinkum-crankum!'*

All the greatest books and movies have a plot twist, an unexpected turn of events that nobody saw coming. In fact, imagine the opposite. Imagine a book or movie with no *crinkum-crankum* …

Darth Vader isn't Luke Skywalker's dad. In actual fact, it turns out that Luke's dad is Henry Skywalker, an accountant with asthma, who gets a kick out of attending virtual meetings.

Charlie Bucket unwraps the chocolate bar and there is no golden ticket so he scrolls on his phone instead.

Harry Potter is just a 10-year-old with a scar on his forehead that he got from falling off his skateboard.

James Bond always dreamt of being a spy but ended up as a shelf stacker at Aldi. He arrives on his pushbike. 007 is his employee number. The end!

How painfully predictable and utterly dull!

A life is not an amazing life without plot twists. Ups and downs. Twists and turns. The turbulence, challenges, strains, sadness, disasters and happy moments. So why not rewrite your story? You're not a victim, imposter or a baddie. You are not a nobody – you very much a somebody. You are the A-lister in the story of your life. There are no disasters or nightmares, just a few unexpected plot twists.

In fact, I've even come up with a title for your autobiography. Scrub that, it's a title for *everyone's* autobiography:

The Crinkum-crankum Kid.

#ArtOfBrillBook #Stuffocation #9010Principle #ChooseDay
#CrinkumCrankum #PlotTwist

ELEVEN: The upside down

Please note....

Yo!

"Everything Speaks"

Welcome to the world of trigger-nometry, which has nothing to do with triangles and everything to do with the science of impact.

ELEVEN moves swiftly on to the game-changing 4-minute rule and an un-funny Knock Knock joke before taking a deep breath and plunging into the most important part of the book.

It's truly a case of now you don't see it, now you do!

Stranger Things fans will know about the upside down, where nothing is quite as it seems. There's something similar in psychology, called inside-out. It's weird because nothing changes, yet everything shifts.

Upside down and inside out? It's stranger than *Stranger Things*!

Trigger-nometry

Another very basic rule of human interaction is that you have an impact on everyone you ever meet. In fact you cannot NOT have an impact. When you walk into a room your presence affects people.

Hence another huge point that screams out from my research: UNDERSTAND YOUR IMPACT.

It works a bit like this:
Trigger
Feeling
Behaviour
Outcome

There are a million things triggering us every day. They make us *feel* a certain way. And our feelings drive our behaviour that, in turn, determines what happens to us – the outcome.

A classic British trigger is the weather. Let's take a cold, dark, rainy Monday morning in February. The alarm goes off and most people crawl out of bed, feeling sluggish and negative, because the weather is awful (again!). So, we feel low. Our behaviour tends to be sluggish and our language negative. There's a lot of huffing and puffing and rolling of eyes. The outcome is that the majority of people have a fair-to-middling day.

A song that comes on the radio, a person, a rude customer, too many emails, some bad news, Friday at 5 pm, Monday at 6 am, a compliment, a text message, your choice of clothes …
they're all triggers.

But – BREAKING NEWS – you are also a trigger. Everything speaks, which means what you say, how you say it, how you walk, how you behave in meetings, what you wear, how you show up in life … everything you ever do is triggering feelings in those around you. And those feelings drive their behaviours that determine their outcomes. To reiterate, you cannot NOT have an impact.

Let me give you a story that's painfully true. When I first got married I was a lecturer at the local college and my wife was a teacher in a school just down the road. We'd get home, exhausted, and I'd ask my wife how her day had been.

I'd then listen to the same story about unruly teenagers, bad behaviour and 'the class from hell', finishing with an exasperated, 'I've had enough of the classroom, when can I retire?'

I spent the first six months of married life biting my tongue and resisting the temptation to remind my wife that's she's 25, so she needs to hang in there for 40 more years. Then, after six months, I stopped listening. I'd heard it all before. I was just waiting for my turn and as soon as my wife paused for breath I was in there … 'You think your day's been bad? Wait till I tell you how bad my day's been … .

We were playing a 'who's had the worst day' competition! And, get this, I loved my job! I was drawn into a habit of negativity, without actually realising it. We were triggering a set of negative feelings in each other. The outcome was a lack of energy and lifelessness, and it was triggering feelings and belief systems in our children, who must have thought work was an awful thing to engage in.

But, like everything, our negativity was just a habit. And habits can change.

Sister Mary decided to change her habit

We swapped our 'who's had the worst day routine' for the 'four-minute rule'. This is a long-held principle of human influence, most beautifully articulated and popularised by Steve McDermott.[27]

Steve tells a story of how he sometimes has to work away from home for up to two weeks at a time. On his return journey he would be travelling for hours and his wife would always let his three children stay up to see their dad. He would open the front door absolutely exhausted after an arduous trip and his kids would launch themselves at him shouting, 'Dad, it's soooo good to see you! Let me tell you about school ... .'

He would reply, often in an exasperated tone, 'No kids, let me tell you about the M25.'

27 McDermott, Steve. (2002). How to be a *Complete and Utter Failure in Life, Work and Everything: Thirty-nine-and-a-half Steps to Lasting Underachievement.* Prentice Hall.

Day after day, Steve would show up in average dad mode until he had an epiphanic thought: *How would the best dad in the world go through that door?*

And that was it. Realising that these were the most important people in his life, he came through the door like the best dad in the world, and the place lit up. Even better, Steve discovered that he only had to do it for four minutes – they'd had enough after that!

The principle is that the first four minutes of every interaction are the most important. I now come through the door with the objective of triggering a positive set of feelings in my family. It's a conscious and determined effort to ditch the old habits of whining, moaning and griping. I ask my children about the highlight of their day, then listen (with fascination) for the answer. Getting home has become a thing of joy and smiles. The children no longer retreat to their rooms while mum and dad swap their low-lights.

Bottom line? The impact you are having on your fellow human beings is profound. So if you're going to have an impact anyway, I think you should strive to make it a positive one, starting four minutes at a time.

It's all inside-out

I'm not gonna lie, I nearly left this bit out but I figure that if you've come this far, you don't just want the golden egg, you want the goose that laid it, so brain in gear, strap yourself in – it's #GoldenGooseTime.

'Just because I can't see it, doesn't mean I can't believe it.'

The Nightmare Before Christmas.

Here's an interesting question to ponder (and, in fact, the question that kick-started my research).

Could you be happier even if nothing in the world around you changed?

My answer, to me, was yes. That was an awakening, a realisation that I had the potential to be happier – nothing needed to change around me – but I wasn't being. It was a clue that the biggest barrier to me feeling amazing, was me.

I'm guessing if I asked you what stresses you out you'd say something like work, deadlines, family, news, the spot on my forehead, what to wear, the weather, what people think about me, the news, my wonky teeth, climate change, mortgage/rent and so on.

And if I asked what makes you happy you'd say weekends, holidays, your family, your cat, ice cream, shopping, fresh air, nature, blue sky, picnics, cake, for example.

These things are making us happy, or sad. Am I right, or am I right?

Actually, *I'm 100% wrong!*

What if I was to tell you that your emotions aren't coming from outside you but rather, every single feeling you've ever felt, and every single feeling you will ever feel, is coming from your thinking – in THIS moment.

You have to let that settle for a while because it changes everything. Inside-out thinking basically means that it's not the person cutting you up in the traffic that's causing you to be angry. It's the way you're *thinking* about the person cutting you up in the traffic.

It's not the weekend that's making you happy. It's the way you're thinking about the weekend.

It's not the person, thing, place or day of the week that's causing your feelings. *You're* causing your feelings. To be precise, the way you're thinking – *right now* – is causing you to feel the way you feel, right now.

Yes, I know it really seems like the world is making you feel angry, sad, jealous, confident, happy, miserable, joyful, grateful … it seems like that to me too. But it's actually the other way around. I'll say it again because when you get it your life will change … *your emotions are coming from your thinking, in this moment.*

They always have and always will. I'm talking about 100% of your feelings, 100% of the time. I appreciate this might be challenging but there are no exceptions!

When you get it, it's like unlocking a new level.

I don't want to push too hard on this because you have to realise it for yourself, but let's step it up by applying inside-out thinking to the past and future.

We've all had bad things happen to us in the past. So, for example, many years ago it's likely you will have had a relationship break up because of something horrible that your partner said or did. You were hurt, angry and embarrassed at the time and those same feelings can well up inside of you right now, decades later.

So, hang on a second, how does that anger and embarrassment time travel from 30 years ago? How does that anger get into my body *right now?* Because I'm *thinking* about that break-up *right now*. I think about it *now* – and I feel it *now* – even though it happened decades ago.

Future? Same! You can get stressed out about an interview that is coming up in three weeks' time. You feel anxious. You can't sleep. But again, how have those nervous feelings time travelled from three weeks in the future to inhabit your body right now? How can something affect you that hasn't even happened yet?

Answer: because you're *thinking* about that interview *right now*.

Top tip

If you keep getting electrocuted it's best to take your fingers out of the socket!

Your emotions are like a special effects department. They bring your thinking to life. Thoughts can be good, bad, sad, angry, jealous, grateful, ungrateful, loving, scary, positive, negative – but whatever they are, you'll be *feeling* them.

It's such a simple concept but the vast majority of people sail through life completely unaware of what I've just revealed. They fall for the illusion and just naturally assume that the outside world is doing things to them.

But inside-out thinking reveals the truth about Mondays, relationships, confidence, meetings, worry, guilt, shame, embarrassment ... everything! The 'problem' isn't the problem. The problem is our misunderstanding about how emotions work.

It's not outside-in, it's *inside-out*. This changes everything because it means the world isn't coming at you, it's coming from you.

Inside-out thinking is humanity's best-kept secret, but here's the paradox – its very simplicity is what makes it hard to grasp. Trust me, I know it absolutely 100% feels like Fridays are making you feel good, an Amazon delivery fills you with joy, an argument with your manager makes you annoyed, a customer complaint makes your blood boil and that a film with a clown makes you terrified ... but if we reveal what's behind the magician's curtain, you'll find it's all just thought weaving its emotional magic.

Inside-out thinking is such a massive deal because the world is very full-on. Things are happening to you all the time, and some of them are BIG things. And because it's a BIG thing, you have some BIG thoughts about it. Most probably anxious, self-conscious, angry, negative, scary ones. If you've having those big thoughts a lot, guess what, you'll be feeling some BIG feelings.

Let me apply it to a simple situation. Imagine that last week you had to do a presentation in a meeting, and speaking in front of everyone is your worst nightmare. You had no choice so you did it, but badly. You were shaky, mumbly and blushing. Presentation finished, you slunk back to your seat.

Today, when you reflect on last week's presentation, you feel embarrassed and shameful. It sure looks like the presentation is dragging you down. Anxious thoughts are swirling around your head while you sit clicking through your emails. *How can I avoid doing presentations in the future? What will people be thinking about me? Why am I so rubbish?*

When you 'get' the true nature of inside-out thinking you realise that the episode happened last week. The presentation is finished. The only way you can feel embarrassed *right now* is because you're thinking about last week's trauma, *right now*.

Apologies for the bluntness, but that presentation is finished. It's history. The only place it's alive is in your thinking, in this moment.

There are two big reveals. First, the trauma is kept alive by your thinking, and second, *you are the thinker.*

Note, I've used the word 'trauma' here because there are genuine traumas that happen to good people. Traditional therapy invites you to think about your trauma, discuss it, reflect on it ... which makes no sense whatsoever because every time you think about it, you are re-living it, and those same terrible emotions are invited back into your body. Some people are in therapy their entire lifetime, re-telling and therefore re-experiencing their childhood traumas.

Inside-out thinking doesn't suggest the trauma never happened, it just reminds you that thinking about it over and over (and over ...) again means you're re-experiencing it over and over (and over ...) again. The terrible event happened, in the past. To repeat the exact same blunt truth from a few sentences ago, that trauma is finished. It's history. The only place it's alive is in your thinking, *in this moment.*

Here's the biggest question in a book of big questions. What if traditional therapy and counselling have got it backwards? The therapists' argument seems to be that you have to revisit your trauma in order to process it. You're encouraged to chat about the pain, maybe re-think how you think about it until you can eventually put the episode behind you.

Common sense tells me the trauma is already behind you! It happened *in the past*. It doesn't make much sense to keep going back to it. I'm pretty sure your trauma was pretty bad at the time so why on earth would you want to re-experience it a thousand times?

I'll come clean with you. Although I understand this, I still sometimes forget. But generally speaking my understanding of inside-out thinking (that my emotions are coming from my thinking *in this moment*) has allowed me to live a calmer life. When I do get grumpy about a late train, or upset by my father-in-law's dementia, or angry about how someone's treated me, inside-out thinking gives me options.

I can:

A) Choose to continue to think grumpy and/or upsetting thoughts (hey, this is the real world. Sometimes it's perfectly okay to have upset feelings).

B) Re-think my thinking and source a more helpful thought.

C) Notice that they're just thoughts. Choose to let the negative ones float past. Don't take them so seriously. Or personally.

D) Understand that this is how *all* human experience is created.

Option A is easy, which is why most people do it. Negative thoughts loop around their head and they stomp through life with hobnailed grumpy boots.

B is useful, but re-thinking your thinking requires some effort.

C is mindfulness. It's *really* useful, but requires some practice to let the critical thoughts float on by.

Option D is a game-changer. You've cracked the code, defeated the end of level boss and moved to the next level. Once you realise that your mind is just doing what minds do – *oh, that's how it works!* – you begin to relax into life. If every feeling is coming from your thinking, right now, it gives you a level of insight that most mortals simply don't have. When your mind jumps in with a bunch of insecure thoughts and feelings (which it will!) you recognise them as nothing to take too seriously. While most people will continue to have a lot on their mind, you'll have less. Once you've got a clearer head, with less mental clutter, it opens up space for solutions, ideas and fresher, nicer thoughts.

> 'Yesterday's the past, tomorrow's the future, but today is a GIFT. That's why it's called the present.'
>
> Master Oogway from Kung Fu Panda (although, to be fair, he borrowed it from others before him)

… and hey presto, positive feelings will flow from the inside-out.

In case you're struggling with this point, let's work the same thing backwards. Think back to happy, joyous times and the chances are they were when you were not thinking about your weaknesses, or the drizzle, or work pressures, or the spot on your chin, or that someone has more social media followers than you do, or the unfairness of life …

That's why things like art, music or sport are great. If you can absorb yourself in a hobby, your thoughts will be focused on something positive and you will feel amazing.

For me, the inside-out understanding boils down to this: do you want peace, or drama?

Remember, you are confident. You are grateful. You are loving and kind. You are all of these things, but with the power to think that you're not. You feel amazing when you realise that you're living in a thought-created 'reality' of you your own making.

It's backwards, but it's the truth.

An awesome version of you is much closer than you think...

TWELVE: Fearing the wurst

BORN
SUPER BUSY
DIED

A terrible sausage pun heralds a banger of a chapter.

Too many people are having a near-life experience, so TWELVE is topped with empathic mimicry and tailed by some words from an old lady, but the main event is sausages.

You're about to be battered. You'll be welcomed to the wonderful world of the sausage machine before falling in love with Norman and Norma at the Sausage Olympics.

Whether you're a red or brown sauce person, get yourself prepped for a sausage fest. Pork ones, veggie ones, life ones ... you're the chef!

Drop dead happy

Everyone knows that owners look like their dogs. We say it as a joke but science bears it out. It's because on a subconscious basis, we choose mutts that are similar to us.

Science has now taken the doppelganger theory further. Guess what, there's evidence to suggest that you may eventually grow to look like your partner?

No, really! Pinky promise. It's called *empathic mimicry*, and it's an actual thing.

Couples who live together for decades tend to have had the same experiences and spend a lot of time in rapport. This matching of emotions on the inside carves out facial features - frowns, anger, grumble mode, laughter lines, whatever - that show up on the outside.

Apparently your facial muscles will be sculpted by time to match those of your long-term partner.

Empathic mimicry. Remember, you heard it here first.

The lesson? *It pays to marry a smiler.*

The Transformers

You don't wake up one day, magically transformed. It's not effortless. In fact I've gone out of my way to tell you that it is not easy (but very worthwhile) work. It's a bit like getting a six-pack stomach. You can't just turn up at the gym once. *There we go, that's me done!*

You have to work at it, and it's very easy to backslide into average mode.

Crafting and maintaining a new improved you represents a degree of personal change. You do things *differently* in the two-percent zone than you do in fair-to-middling mode. And, breaking news, nobody's going to change your habits for you. YOU have to take charge of it.

Herein lies a point that doesn't always land well. I'll call it 'taking personal responsibility'.

Those at the upper end of the wellbeing graph tend not to play the blame game. If things aren't working out they are big enough to point the finger back at themselves and say, 'OK, what can I do to get an outcome? How can I change something about me to influence the situation?'

I like Richard Wilkins' analogy of life as a sausage machine. It fits perfectly. I recommend you book yourself onto one of Richard's Broadband Consciousness courses to hear about the sausage machine first hand.

The principle is deadly simple. In a sausage machine, there's a direct correlation between what you put in and what you get out.

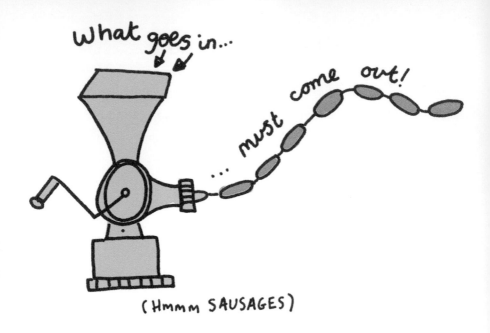

What goes in...

... must come out!

(Hmmm SAUSAGES)

To get pork sausages, most sane people would agree that they'd have to put pork into the sausage machine in the first place. And if you wanted vegetarian sausages you'd have to put ~~vegetarians~~ *vegetables* in.

And, just to ram the point home, you wouldn't put beef in and expect vegan sausages to come out of the other end. That'd be stupid. You'd be waiting a very long time.

I have a phobia of German sausage.

Yes, I fear the wurst.

(My only sausage joke)

Now substitute the sausage machine for life and think about your ingredients. Are they the right ones, because my point about 'personal responsibility' is that it's your life and they're your ingredients. Too many people are putting in low energy, can't-be-bothered, negativity and a grumbling habit. They stick these kinds of ingredients into their sausage machine of life and wonder why life is dealing them a doom, gloom, low energy, counting-down-to-the-weekend kind of life. It's a simple rule – garbage in, garbage out.

To use Richard Wilkins' terminology – are you the waiter, or creator? Too many people are at the wrong end of the sausage machine of life. They're at the sausage end – waiting and waiting and waiting (and waiting, and hoping ...) for life to become amazing. Once the personal responsibility penny drops you move to the ingredients end, and take charge of putting good stuff into your life.

How about these for ingredients ... energy, enthusiasm, confidence, positivity, kindness, gratitude, 'can do', exuberance, happiness and smiles? These are just random ingredients that come to mind, but I tell you what, life would deal you some fabulous sausages!

Kummerspeck (German):
Excess weight gained from emotional overeating.
Literally, 'grief bacon'.

The Norms

I love the Olympics. It rocks up every four years and I'm sucked into watching sports I didn't even know existed! Dancing horses, ribbon twirling gymnastics, swimming in formation, BMX, hop/skip/jump, going for a brisk hip-waggling walk ... I'm addicted.

Even though I might not understand the rules, I watch in awe because the Olympics is the very best against the very best. But because they're all superb, we, the viewer, can lose perspective. We know Mr Fast is fast and that he'll beat the other not-quite-so-fast sprinters by 0.01 of a second. We know an 80-metre javelin throw is a very long way and two saltos backwards with three twists in a tucked position is astonishing, but when they're *all* doing it, it can lose its awesomeness.

With that in mind, I've got an idea to improve what is already the best show on earth. I'm calling it the 'Sausage Machine Olympics'.

In order for us to understand just how good the competitors are, I'm recommending that every event has an average person. Selected from millions of candidates, hand-picked for their bog-standardness, let's call them Norma and Norman, aka, 'the Norms', and they have to compete in every event.

Please take a moment to picture Norman … cheap suit, slight belly, slumped shoulders, exhausted eyes, likes a trip to the pub, hybrid job that splits his time between his kitchen table and an empty office, eats pizza, has dandruff and that overworked haggard look about him.

And Norma? Same, but with muffin tops and a badly fitting bra.

Picture the scene. The stadium is jam-packed for the blue ribbon event. As Mr Fast and all those other not-quite-so-fasts stretch their chests at the 100-metre finish line, Norman is rising from the blocks.

As Ms Swim stretches her exhausted fingers towards the end of the 50-metre butterfly sprint, Norma is adjusting her goggles and easing down the ladder into the shallow end.

As Mr Javelin hurls his spear over the 85-metre line, Norman mistimes his and accidentally spears one of the judges.

Norma returns from a cheeky vape break and nervously waits her turn in the gymnastics hall. Two saltos backwards with three twists in a tucked position is a tough act to follow, but she does her best, thundering down the padded runway and leap-frogging the horse, like she used to do at school. She pops out of her badly fitting bra but is proud to have stayed on her feet.

There are serious points to my new Sausage Machine Olympic rules.

First, it's easy to be one of the Norms. It takes no training or dedication to achieve averageness. Bog standard is indeed the standard.

Think of the ingredients that are needed to achieve 'world class'. I'm using a silly Olympic story to make the point but you're clever enough to realise it's not about sport, or indeed, Norman and Norma.

It's about life, and you. If there was an Olympics for attitude, positivity, optimism, enthusiasm, passion, resilience and happiness – would you be a Norm?

If so, I'd like you to raise your sights to gold-medal standard. Be the creator, not the waiter.

Welcome to the world of the two-percenters, where rising above average means you'll stand out for all the right reasons.

Consider the following,
written by Nadine Stair, aged 85

I'd dare to make more mistakes next time.

I'd relax, I'd limber up.

I would have been sillier than I have been on this trip.

I would take fewer things seriously.

I would take more chances.

I would take more trips.

I would climb more mountains and swim more rivers. I would eat more ice creams and fewer veggies.

I would perhaps have more actual troubles but I'd have fewer imaginary ones.

You see, I'm one of those people who live sensibly and sanely hour after hour, day after day.

Oh, I've had my moments and if I had to do it over again, I'd have more of them. In fact, I'd try to have nothing else. Just moments.

If I had my life over, I would start barefoot earlier in the spring and stay that way later in the autumn.

I would go to more dances.

I would ride more merry-go-rounds.

I would pick more daisies.

I've been one of those people who never go anywhere without a thermometer, a hot water bottle, a raincoat and a parachute.

If I had to do it again, I would travel lighter next time. But, you see, I don't get a second chance.

#ArtOfBrillBook #EmpathicMimicry #SausageMachine #NormAndNorma

Hey!

THIRTEEN:
No hard feelings

This chapter introduces you to the original Spider-Man (who wore tartan, not Lycra) and then brings you seven words that will change your life. I could have stopped right there but, no, you also get a human-being repair kit and a wonderfully (almost) true story about a horse with a liking for pizza.

You'll learn some new lingo – look out for *vipassana vendetta* and *maladaptive stress response* – and there's a generous helping of hippos and hugs.

Starting with an emotional rollercoaster and ending with an NLP anchoring technique, this chapter has resilience at its core.

'Sometimes you're the windshield;

Sometimes you're the bug'

MARK KNOPFLER (ROCK STAR)

It's okay NOT to be okay

The following diagram represents someone whose emotions are all over the place. However, if you measure this individual over six months, they are actually in the two-percenter bracket. Most of their time is spent feeling pretty damn fine, but this was a particularly tough week.

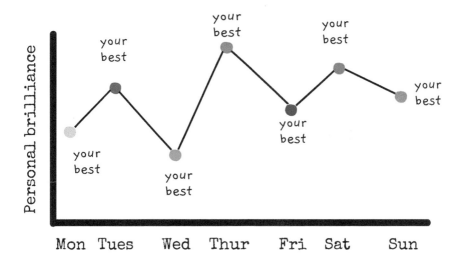

Looking at the chart you'll see that Wednesday beat them up!

The good news is that this emotional rollercoaster is perfectly normal. Everyone – even the happiest people you know – will have weeks like this. It's okay to NOT be okay isn't a cliché, it's the truth.

'The truth for sure, when it arrives, will make you smile. If it doesn't, you should seek a deeper truth.'

Terence Mckenna.
America ethnobotanist.

The trick is to recognise it, acknowledge it and have the wherewithal to bounce back (which, looking at the chart, is what they did on Thursday!).

Spider-Man, origin.

The year is 1314. The place, Bannockburn, Scotland. Robert the Bruce is going toe-to-toe with the English and although his men are outnumbered by 10 to 1, he's kicking ass.

Yes, at odds of 10 to 1, *against!*

There's a statue of him at Stirling Castle. For the Scots, Robert the Bruce is a legend.

For the English, he's someone we give a grudging nod of respect, and learn from. If you rewind to a decade before his famous Bannockburn victory, you'd have found Robert the Bruce and his army taking a beating on the blood-soaked battlefield of Strath-Fillan.

Defeated, RtB escaped and went into hiding in a cave. Cold, wet, exhausted and bleeding from his wounds, he felt utterly hopeless. So great was his shame and so crushing his despair, he thought about leaving Scotland and never returning.

But as he lay there he looked up and noticed a spider that was trying to spin a web across a gap in the wall of the cave. This was no easy task. The spider would spin a strand and string it from one side of the gap to the other. Then it would spin another and another, weaving back and forth to build the web. But every few minutes a strong gust of wind would blow through the gap, breaking the web and sending the spider tumbling.

Pretty frustrating for Incy Wincy, but Robert noticed that the spider refused to give up. The moment the wind died down, it would crawl back up to the edge of the gap and start spinning again, from scratch. Time after time the wind blew the web apart, and time after time the spider started re-spinnning.

Eventually, the wind died down long enough for the spider to spin a firm enough foundation, so that the next time the wind kicked up the web was strong enough to withstand it, and the spider was finally able to finish the job.

Robert the Bruce was amazed by this spider's persistence. The spider became his personal symbol of inspiration and he coined the famous motto, *If at first you don't succeed, try, try again.*

Probably the only great leader to be inspired by a spider, after his wounds had healed, RtB raised another army, marched them to Bannockburn and the rest, as they say, is history.

Change your life in seven words

'I really think a champion is defined not by their wins, but by how they can recover when they fall.'

Serena Williams. Tennis superstar.

There are times when you're perfectly within your rights to feel sorry for yourself. My mate Professor Paul McGee[28] suggests that humans should learn a lesson from hippos. From time to time, we all need a good wallow.

So #BeMoreHippo. Have a bad day. *Enjoy* your wallow! Hippo Time is a necessary and important part of your journey, but please take a moment to digest the Prof.'s next point ...

---

28 McGee, Paul. (2015). *Shut Up, Move On: The Straight-Talking Guide to Succeeding in Life.* Capstone.

Wallowing is *not* your final destination. You've got to find the courage to haul yourself out of the swamp. Mental strength is about getting back in the game. It's about having a positive mindset, learning from failure, making good choices *(consistently)* and spending your energy wisely.

It's worth reminding you of this – sometimes the bravest thing you will ever do is ask for help. If you think about it, asking for help is a sign of remarkable courage. It's a signal that you're refusing to give up.

Ask for help...

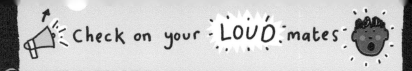
Check on your LOUD mates

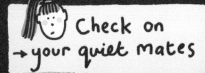
Check on your quiet mates

Check on your 'always Ok' mate ok!

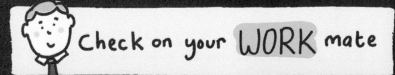
Check on your **grumbly** mate

Check on your **SICK** mate

Check on your healthy mate

Check on your WORK mate

Check on your flat mate

Check on your **BEST** mate

Check on yourself, mate
#checkmate

Here are seven words that changed my life. It doesn't sound like a life-changing sentence, but I promise you, it is.

Do it better than you have to.

And by 'it' I mean 'everything'.

Put more effort in than you have to.
Be kinder than you have to.
Eat a bit healthier than you have to.
Be a better friend than you have to.
Work a bit harder than you have to.
Care a bit more than you have to.
Go to bed a bit earlier than you have to.
Visit your in-laws a bit more regularly than you have to.
Hug your children a bit more frequently (and for a few seconds longer) than you have to.
Be a better listener than you have to.

… you get the point.

All these *little bit better than you have to*s add up to the difference between YOU 1.0 and YOU 2.0. It's not about making dramatic changes. I'm suggesting you start doing lots of little things a bit better than you did them yesterday. And tomorrow, a teensy weensy bit better again.

And again.
And again.
And again.
And again.

And again …

It's about small improvements in attitude and behaviour every single day. I think you'll really enjoy the upgrade and, guess what, these changes start to become normal, they get grooved into your habits and, hey presto, there's an everyday superhero staring back at you while you brush your teeth.

Bonus Tip: How to repair a broken human

Humans are all made of flesh and blood, with emotions, dreams, hopes, fears and insecurities. We're built to certain specifications so are able to withstand the normal wear and tear of life, but remember, the pressures of the modern world are considerable.

'Money can buy you a fine dog, but only love can make him wag his tail.'

Kinky Friedman. American singer, songwriter and politician.

People do actually break – and that's fine. It's to be expected. Your family and friends don't come with a receipt. If they're wilting under the strain, or if they have developed a fault, or have actually broken, you can't take them back to the shop and swap them for a new one.

But here's a sure-fire 100% guaranteed way to help fix a broken relative or friend.

To put the love back into their hearts, you must administer a magical seven-second hug. Note, the average hug lasts 2.1 seconds so seven seconds is really stretching it. Which is exactly the point. Sometimes your loved ones need a pick-me-up so a seven-second hug, plus an 'I love you' and/or 'I'm sorry and I mean it' is a wonderful explosion of genuine affection. It heals almost anything.

HUG DEALER

Hug Dealer small print
Seven seconds is an I ♥ U hug. No words are necessary. Seven seconds is just long enough for the other person to know that you love them. It contains life-changing properties but should only be administered to very close family and friends. It's absolutely NOT for strangers in the park because that would be weird. Never count out loud because it spoils the effect. You don't actually have to wait for your siblings, parents, gran or bestie to look jaded before you do the seven-second hug thing. They provide an instant boost pretty much anytime. Warning: seven seconds is advanced hugging. Those who are already huggy will absolutely love the full seven seconds but you'll be able to spot the non-huggers – they start wriggling and you have to cling on for the love to transfer. Good luck!

Horses for courses.
It's the last line that counts ...

I live near a man who owns some horses. It just so happened that the school bus stopped right at the gate to his horses' field and, while he was at work, the school children would get off the bus and feed them their scraps.

The horses loved it! Mars bars, crisps and stuff the kids had made in cooking. The horses developed a taste for pepperoni pizza. Over time, the horses got fat. So the man put up a sign that said, 'Do not feed the horses.'

Did it work? Did it heck!

The feeding frenzy continued, so the owner changed the sign. It now read, 'PLEASE do not feed the horses!'

His problem continued until I bumped into him at a school fête. He knew I was a positive psychology enthusiast so explained the problem in the hope of getting a simple solution. 'How on earth can I stop the kids feeding my horses?'

I chuckled and wrote him a few words on a scrap of paper. The man looked at the paper and laughed. 'No way!'

I smiled a knowing smile and the problem was cured.

The horses are now back to their normal weight, their coats shining and energy restored. If you saunter past their field there is now a sign that says, 'We only eat apples and carrots.'

The message is simple and positive. It focuses on what we want to happen rather than what we don't want. And, best of all, it works.

Get the communication right and the results will follow, remembering of course that the most important person you ever communicate with is yourself!

The bouncebackability button

> 'The flower that blooms in adversity is the most rare and beautiful of all.'
>
> Emperor of China. Mulan

Before I get stuck into this section, I need you to be grown up enough to understand that too many people are generating their own stress. I'm not necessarily pointing the finger at you, but if you look around, and listen in, you'll hear people overreacting on a massive scale.

'Vipassana vendetta' is a beautiful mash-up of Buddhism and Hinduism that translates as *the magnification of minor irritations into full blown anger*. This is when someone's giving it the full histrionics of, 'Oh my gosh this is my worst nightmare' when, in actual fact, their train has been cancelled. While a cancelled train isn't ideal, if it's your worst nightmare, you are living a charmed life. Translating vipassana vendetta into modern psychological parlance, you are creating a maladaptive stress response. Your brain is treating a terse email like a prowling wolf. The emergency sirens go off between your ears and your body is hijacked by cortisol.

So please beware of when you're falling foul of pressing the over-reaction self-destruct button. You need to notice, take a deep breath and chill. It's a negative remark, a bad driver, a rude person or someone's unfollowed you on social media. It is not a snarling hungry wolf.

That said, I would be lying if I told you that by choosing to be positive and taking responsibility for putting superb ingredients into your sausage machine, every day will be filled with unicorns and rainbows. Let's get real. There are times when life can be – how can I put this gently – despicably and unspeakably shit.

Unfairly so.

There are loads of examples of life situations where, quite frankly, it wouldn't be appropriate to be upbeat and positive so, rest easy, even happy people experience extreme grief and sadness.

 But they tend to not get stuck there because they have what I call 'bouncebackability' or what is more commonly known as 'resilience'. Their habits lie in the upper quartile of wellbeing, but life will deal them some bad things and they will experience negative emotions.

Bouncebackability is the hardest of the two-percenter traits.

> 'There are two ways to live: you can live as if nothing is a miracle; you can live as if everything is a miracle.'
>
> Albert Einstein.
> The E=MCsquared guy

When life's dealt you a redundancy or marriage break-up, or when someone you love passes away, then it's very hard to bounce back. The two-percenters manage it largely because they've chosen to be positive and so they know that the current situation is not permanent. There is a grieving period, but they move forward positively rather than dwelling in the mire. Someone in best-self mode will remain focused on the solution rather than the problem, and the future rather than the now.

There are various neuro-linguistic techniques that will help you bounce back, of which 'anchoring' is probably the simplest. Once again, in terms of keeping things understandable, I'll provide a quick technique that I sometimes do in my school workshops. I call it the 'Bouncebackability Button'.

Read the passage and then close your eyes and do it. Remember – eyes closed, but mind wide open!

Think of a time when you felt invincible. A time when you felt like you could take on the world. Maybe it was your wedding day, a superb family holiday, winning an award, or your best ever tee shot. Remember back to that time and run the movie in your mind. Turn up the colours and sounds. Run it forwards, choosing to slow it down at the moments when your brilliant feelings peaked. It's your movie. They are your memories and feelings. This is the Director's Cut.

Now open your eyes and find a felt tipped pen. Draw a circle on the back of your hand. Close your eyes and run the movie again. The same as before but turn the colours up even brighter. Magnify the feelings. Then magnify them again. Feel the brilliance flowing through you. Confidence. Happiness. Love. Positive. Goodness me, isn't it great to be alive?

As the feelings reach a crescendo, gently press on the circle. Press just a little bit harder and hold while you run the main event of the movie. Let the feelings flow into your Bouncebackability Button.

And that's all there is to it. If this is the first time you have done this kind of thing it may feel a bit weird, but you've just anchored yourself into a positive state. I advise the Bouncebackability Button is pressed in emergencies only. It's not for when the traffic lights are on red – it's for when life deals you some serious stuff and you need a short boost to get through a situation. Maybe at an interview or to give confidence before a presentation. It only takes a second. Press the back of your hand and recall the time when you felt 10-feet tall and bulletproof. The good feelings are released and you'll feel much more capable of handling whatever life has dealt you.

Like I say, emergencies only please. Don't wear out your Bouncebackability Button!

#ArtOfBrillBook #RobertTheBruce #SpiderMan #7Words
#DoItBetterThanYouHaveTo #7SecondHug #Bouncebackability

FOURTEEN: HUGE goals and BIG strengths

I can hardly type 'SMART' without my eyes rolling to the back of my head and froth foaming from my mouth. It's a form of corporate and personal sabotage. Why would you condemn yourself to a life of mediocrity?

This chapter teaches you to SUPERSIZE your life by going large on your dreams. You'll be introduced to the coolest goal-setting technique the world has ever seen but, of course, if you're aiming for the stratosphere, you'll be needing to play to your strengths.

This chapter finishes with the parable of Clarence and Felix.
Does it work, not sure?
Is it any good, possibly not?
Was it fun writing it? *Hell yes!*

But first, to set the scene, here's Tamsin ...

Bonus Story: ONE Life

Tamsin's been lucky enough to visit the San Fermin Festival in Pamplona, España. Tens of thousands of people gather for the main event, the release of 40 raging bulls that rampage through the streets. Some festival goers jump over the barriers and run with the herd. If you survive (and some don't!) you have memories that are etched forever. The vast majority of people are happy to watch.

What would you do, and why?

Tamsin's also been lucky enough to visit the Grand Canyon, USA. Hundreds of thousands of people arrive in coaches, stand on the edge of the chasm and gawp at the one-mile vertical drop. Then they eat their sandwiches, get back on their air-conditioned bus and drive to Vegas. A handful lace up their boots, pack their backpacks and venture downward, following a rocky path, until they reach the gushing Colorado river. They set up camp, before hiking back up the next day.

What would you do, and why?

Along with another eight billion lottery winners, Tamsin's been lucky enough to have won a ticket to life. Every day she squeals with delight because she knows the odds of being born are squillions to one. Tamsin gets stuck in, prioritising happiness and adventure. She does stuff and seeks out new places. Tamsin marvels at the seasons, jumps in puddles and grins a lot. But the vast majority seem content to sink into mediocrity. Their days drag and their sparkle is reserved for holidays and weekends.

If you had a choice, what would you do, and why?

Hey, it's not absolutely clear-cut but, on balance, I think the message is #BeMoreTamsin

Why SMART is stupid

There's an awful lot of nonsense written about goal setting. David Taylor demystifies it in his brilliant book, *The Naked Leader*[29] by distilling it down into the following four stages:

'Everyone says you should follow your dreams, so I'm going back to bed.'

Aunty Acid.
A Ged Backland cartoon creation.

Work out where you are now.
Work out where you want to be.
Work out what you have to do to get there.
Do it!

I could cull this chapter right here because he's nailed it, but here are a few how-tos …

It's important to understand that 'success' isn't a straight line. It looks rather like a plate of spaghetti bolognaise – you stick your fork in, whirl it around and slurp some in.

It's a bit hit and miss and, yes, success is messy!

In terms of achieving amazing things in your life, my advice is to take a lesson from my research into two-percenters – ditch SMART and GO LARGE. And small.

Confused? Let me explain.

---

29 Taylor, David. (2002). *The Naked Leader.* Capstone.

First of all, just because you're taught to set SMART objectives on every management course ever, doesn't mean it's right. I won't trot out the entire acronym for fear of boring myself, but I have a particular bone to pick with the 'Achievable' and 'Realistic' parts. Suffice to say I cannot think of a single breakthrough in human kind that would ever have been achieved if we'd pitched in at achievable and realistic.

You should supersize your goals. Here it is in a single sentence: If you want to achieve amazing things in your life, then you have to elevate to HUGGs – Huge Unbelievably Great Goals.

A HUGG is something that inspires and excites you. It's on the edges of your achievability. It's something that isn't going to happen by accident; it happens because you make it happen.

You have to step into best-self mode and ask yourself some searching questions:

First, what do you want to achieve in the next year, two, maybe five years? Clue: it has to be something edgy, exciting and worth getting out of bed for.

Second, you visualise your huge goal in great detail. What does it look, sound and feel like? Smell it. Taste it. Snuggle into the feeling of having achieved it.

Third, what are the steps to getting to where you want to be?

And last, have you got the courage to take some action?

Here's the HUGG pyramid that was introduced to me by the goal setting guru, David Hyner.[30] It literally changed my life.

30 Check Dave out at https://www.davidhyner.com/. The man's a legend.

HUGGy instructions

You start at the top. The only rule is that what you write as your Huge Unbelievably Great Goal has to have the wow-factor. It has to ignite the fire in your belly.

Once you're worked out what your HUGG is, it's game on. The thing about HUGE goals is exactly that. They're MASSIVE! In fact they might be so GINORMOUS that it's hard to know where to start, so the next step is to go to the bottom layer of your pyramid and start to fill in the small things that you have to do every *single day* that will move you forward.

We call the individual blocks SUGGs; Small Unbelievably Great Goals. The bottom layer is all about daily habits. It's about creating the version of you that shows up every day.

Then fill in the things you have to do to get 'half way' and 'nearly there'. Give it some serious thought. Fill in *all* the blanks. Colour them in!

Own them!

With all the sections of the pyramid filled in, stick the thing on your fridge and look at it every day. Something exciting will be staring right back at you, the massive goal and the steps to achieving it.

No excuses! *It'll be in your own handwriting!*

Here's a point that's bigger than it seems. Often, you are kept away from your huge bucket-list goals, not by obstacles, but by a clear path to a lesser goal. Read that again (and again) until it sinks in!

I've heard it called the Law of GOYA: Get Off Your Ass! Huge goals provide you with a powerful cocktail of willpower (which gets you off your backside) and *way*-power (which gives you something magnificent to aim for so you *stay* off your backside!).

Note, it's not plain sailing. You have to become someone who's happy to live what I call a cha-cha life – taking a step backward after taking a step forward is *not* a disaster.

Bottom line? For too many, the human race is a lifetime sprint towards mediocrity. Quit that particular race. Stop wasting your motivation on small stuff.

Get committed. Go LARGE.

HUGGs and SUGGs. They'll take you one step beyond.

It's goal-setting MADNESS.

Get bothered!

But there's more. Ultimately, the difference between setting one of those normal boring SMART objectives or a HUGG boils down to this: in terms of goals, are you interested or committed?

For example, you can be *interested* in writing your book, you can be *interested* in studying for a professional qualification, you can be *interested* in developing your own app, you can be *interested* in starting your own business, you can be *interested* in running your

'A little less conversation, a bit more action!'

Elvis Presley.
The king of rock 'n' roll

first marathon, you can be *interested* in working hard, you can be interested in being your best self ...

My point? There are a lot of people *interested* in achieving amazing things. The talkers.

HUGGs are for the *seriously committed*. The doers.

Remember, it's easy to play small. The Jonah Principle from Chapter Nine suggested it's easy to NOT achieve your full potential. It's easy to talk yourself out of going for your dreams – *it's too difficult, I'm not clever enough, it'll take too long, what if I fail?*

So in addition to creating your super-powerful HUGG pyramid you might need to change your words. Here are two surprisingly powerful questions that hardly anyone ever asks ...

1. What kind of person do I need to be to achieve my huge unbelievable great goal?
2. What am I willing to give up to achieve my huge unbelievable great goal?

I'll leave those biggies hanging while I dispense some advice that goes against everything you've ever been taught.

In the interests of challenging you ... come closer 'cos I've got to whisper it ...

... *you need to stop trying!*

Please note, I'm choosing my words very carefully here. For the record, I'm all for effort. The 'EF-word' is not just an ingredient in success – it's *the* ingredient.

So please aim for an A for effort. But a Z in trying.

But the word 'try' ruins everything!

My life has blossomed ever since I cut it out of my vocabulary. Unbeknown to me, that niggly little word had wheedled its way into my book of excuses. I had the best of intentions. I was most definitely a trier. I'd tell myself things like:

I'll *try* to get my book written, I'll *try* to get in shape, I'll *try* to eat healthier, I'll try to go to bed earlier, I'll *try* to be more confident ...

And I'd fail every time because of that piddling three-letter word!

So I ditched it. I literally stopped trying. That was 20 years ago, and to this day, I still don't try, and my life is epic!

If you go back to the sentences above and delete the word try, they read thus:
I'll get my book written.
I'll get in shape.
I'll eat healthier.
I'll go to bed earlier.
I'll be more confident.

All of a sudden, the words have changed from wishy-washy, lily-livered, half-baked things I'd quite like to do, into steadfast promises I'm absolutely going to do.

I've gone from interested to committed.

'Success is neither magical nor mysterious. Success is the natural consequence of consistently applying basic fundamentals.'

Jim Rohn. Author and motivational speaker.

Supersize your strengths

If you're going large on your goals, it also makes sense to supersize your strengths.

There has been some exciting research in recent times, led by luminaries such as Alex Linley, Marcus Buckingham and Tom Rath around the concept of signature strengths. Once again, I'll distil the research into its simplest form (thankfully the principle is relatively straightforward anyway).

Basically, you've got a much better chance of feeling fantastic if you're in an occupation where you're given plenty of scope to play to your strengths. You intuitively know this to be true without me having to hammer it home. You know that you come alive when you're challenged in just the way you like to be challenged. You've got skills that someone's recognised and you are bringing them to the fore every day. As Marcus Buckingham says in one of his excellent videos, these are times when 'work doesn't feel like work'. It's akin to Csikszentmihalyi's concept of flow. Time flies. You're totally absorbed in whatever it is you're doing. You don't feel exhausted. On the contrary, you feel refreshed and invigorated!

So playing to your strengths makes you come alive! If we know this to be true, why do most organisations send people on courses to plug their weaknesses? Why do we recruit people because of their strengths and then carry out appraisals to find their Achilles heel?

Take me as an example. As a junior manager I once had a 360-degree appraisal. That means everyone had the chance to stick their oar in, even my customers! I was summoned for feedback.

Yikes!

I'm proud to say that most of it was glowing. I was rated very highly in 24 of the 25 categories. I sat there grinning. 'But,' my manager warned, 'this red box is your weakest area. Spreadsheets. You obviously don't know how to use Excel', he said, pointing at the evidence in the report.

'Ex what?' I said. I'd never heard of it. I was a trainer so didn't need to use Excel. PowerPoint was my thing.

'Spreadsheets, he continued. 'They allow you to calculate things. They use them in accounts a lot.'

'Thank goodness I'm not in accounts then', I chucked in a pally kind of way. 'Cos my other scores are great.'

But he couldn't get past the Excel issue. My personal action plan was, you've guessed it, to enrol on an Excel spreadsheets course! Which demoralised and frustrated the hell out of me.

There's absolutely no doubt that their money would have been better spent developing me in areas where I was already pretty good. I'd have got excited about going on a wellbeing course, or learning about mindfulness. Whoopee! I'd have bounced out of my 360 review singing the organisation's praises, rather than sulking like a naughty child.

Businesses the world over are making the same mistakes. Maybe, just maybe, we can turn conventional thinking on its head by realising you will get more value from your training budget by breaking with tradition and spending time and money developing your people in areas they're already good at!

Jenny was so good at shot-put that she decided to go for the marathon as well.

Ideally, Jenny needs to be same height, but very chunky, I guess, brings me back to weaknesses. What are we supposed to do about them? Ignore them and hope they'll go away? Erm, no. My advice on weaknesses is to be aware of them. Plug them if they are stopping you performing your job safely or competently, but other than that, chill. Everyone has weaknesses. What you'll find is that successful people focus on their strengths rather than their weak areas.

They succeed *despite* their weaknesses.

The parable of Clarence and Felix

To tie HUGGs and strengths together here's the tale of one man and his frog. Sit back and relax into the utter ridiculousness of Clarence and Felix …

Once upon a time there lived a man named Clarence who had a pet frog named Felix. Clarence was a dreamer who lived a modest existence on what he earned working at the Cash and Carry.

'Ureka!' he exclaimed one day, 'Felix, we're going to be rich! You're gonna be an amphibian phenomenon. I'm going to make you into a social media sensation by teaching you how to fly!'

Felix raised an eyebrow from his bowl of flies. From where he was sitting, it sounded like a bad idea.

On the first day of flying lessons, Clarence could barely control his excitement (and Felix could barely control his bladder). Clarence explained that their apartment had 15 floors, and each day Felix the frog would jump out of a window, starting with the first floor and eventually getting to the top floor. Clarence would record it on his phone, post it on social and analyse the results.

'The world's first-ever flying frog', he said, bit-coin signs in his eyes as he thought of all the clicks. 'Felix old buddy, you're about to go viral!'

Felix pleaded for his life, but his desperate ribbeting fell on deaf ears. Clarence pressed record, and threw Felix out of the first floor window. The YouTube upload showed a terrified amphibian landing with a thud.

Day two, bandaged up and poised for his second flying lesson, Felix begged not to be thrown out of the window. With that, Clarence opened his pocket guide to 'Managing More Effectively' and showed Felix the part about how one must always expect resistance when implementing change. 'People don't like change, and neither do frogs', he said. And, with that, he threw Felix out of the second floor window.

Plop!

On the third day, Felix tried a different ploy. Stalling, he asked for a delay in the project until better weather made flying conditions more favourable.

But no – *whump* – he was tossed out into the storm.

On day four, Clarence had prepared a PowerPoint with the results to date. He was disappointed to announce that there had only been three clicks and a single comment that caused Felix to raise an eyebrow in acknowledgment: U gonna kill dat frog! But Clarence remained upbeat, beaming a picture of rhacophorus nigropalmatus, aka, a flying frog from the Amazon. 'You see! Flying frogs do exist. If you can buy them from Amazon', he said, 'it must be possible to train you.'

Now, understand that Felix really was trying his best. On the fifth day he flapped his legs madly in a vain attempt to stay in the air. On the sixth day he tied a small red cape around his neck and tried to think 'Superfrog' thoughts but, try as he might, Felix couldn't fly.

By day seven Felix, accepting his fate, no longer begged for mercy. 'Shut up and open the window', he ribbeted quietly. The frog eased himself forward on his crutches, took in the seventh floor view and fell, taking careful aim for the large jagged rock by the car park.

It was a messy affair but Felix got his wish and went to that great lily pad in the sky.

Clarence was upset. His get-rich-quick project had failed to meet a single goal and there had been zero improvement in the seven days despite Clarence commanding the frog to, 'Fall smarter, not harder.' Even worse, #AmphibianPhenomenon and #FlyingFrog were anything but viral.

The only thing left for Clarence to do was analyse the process and try to determine where it had gone wrong. After much thought, Clarence smiled. 'Bingo!' he said, 'Next time, I'm getting a smarter frog!'

How might this story relate to your workplace?

_____

_____

_____

_____

_____

_____

Relating Clarance and Felix to the themes of this chapter (goals and strengths) what's the moral of this story?

_____

_____

_____

_____

_____

_____

_____

#ArtOfBrillBook #BeMoreTamsin #HUGGs #SUGGs #Botheredness
#ChaChaLife #ClarenceAndFelix

FIFTEEN: Omnipotent handstands

It's the final instalment, so we've pulled out all the stops and dusted off our most requested story. Plot spoiler #BeMoreSeb

Then, to finish, it's not one but TWO trips to Heaven. I go first, with a whimsical piece about The Cloud, but my co-author has the final word. If you Google 'nested loop' (like I just have), it describes them as: when you start telling a story, a metaphor, or an anecdote, get some of the way through it and stop (leaving the audience in suspense) before starting another story.

Hey, I doubt Andy's 'Can God do a handstand?' story left you in suspense, but it does need finishing. Then we'll be out of your face and you can get on with living your BEST life.

For whom the bridge tolls
Embellished, but based on a true story.

There's a toll bridge, somewhere in America. Let's say it's somewhere sunny and warm and there are 10 lanes of traffic. It costs five dollars to cross the bridge and, to be honest, it's not the most inspiring of jobs. The toll collectors spend their shift cooped up in a small cubicle, taking the five bucks, and pressing a button to lift the barrier. It's repetitive and monotonous. Understandably, most employees go through the motions, zombie-like, wishing their time away.

Except one. Seb occupies lane ten, and Seb *loves* coming to work. In fact, he brings his Bluetooth speaker, cranks up the volume and has a party every day.

Seb sings, dances and beams his way through every eight-hour shift.

Seb has got to know his regulars and he exchanges some banter and well-wishing as they pass through lane ten.

'Have a great day, Mr B.'

'Say "hi" to the kids, Marianne.'

'Welcome to lane ten. Isn't it a glorious day?' he grins at the next customer. 'Seeing as it's your first time with me, I'd advise you to drive quite slowly across the bridge. Get your five dollars' worth, what with the beautiful view and all. And, sir, if you're ever in the neighbourhood again, I'd be honoured to serve you in lane ten next time. Have a fabulous day.'

The staff going through the motions in one to nine take the customers' cash with anodyne efficiency. Work is a chore. They wish they weren't there.

Seb in lane ten stands out a mile!

And here's the rub – if you cross the bridge after the rush hour's subsided and the queues have dwindled – you will notice a strange phenomenon. Lanes one to nine are empty. The toll operators are strumming their fingers as they wait for their next customer, their lives ticking away until home time.

And yet lane ten has a queue. Seb has his devotees. These are people who prefer to queue for a few minutes to pay their five dollars to Seb, rather than breeze through lanes one to nine.

If you can work out why, our work here is done.

Now you've read our book, you should have enough information to change your life for the better. If you put what you have learned into practice, you will move into the top two-percent bracket. You will join the merry band of stand-out humans, which means you've got a stronger chance of having a flourishing life.

Guaranteed, *no*. Better odds, *yes*.

The book has been crafted around six principles, which are all there for the taking. Let's revise them, and remember, although they look mightily simple their DNA comes from my doctoral research.

Choose to be positive.
Understand your impact.
Take personal responsibility.
Have bouncebackability.
Set Huge Goals.
Play to your strengths.

Is there anything above that you cannot do? Or anything dreadfully complex that you can't fathom?

No? Then may we respectfully ask that you go and do them. It just takes a little effort.

> 'Change will not come if we wait for some other person or some other time. We are the ones we've been waiting for. We are the change that we seek.'
>
> Barack Obama. Former US President.

WARNING! This is NOT a dream!

It's curious that despite our lack of religious fervour, Andy and I have both gone for spiritual endings.

Me first. I kicked the book off with one of The Specials' song titles, *Enjoy yourself, it's later than you think*, so I'll finish off on the same theme.

With eternity stretching into the past and future, an average earthly existence of 4000 weeks can seem a bit measly. We can become saddled with this thing called life expectancy, counting down until D-day.
Another day gone, another week slips by, another month ticked off …

It's easily done and even easier to live a *coulda, shoulda, woulda life* of *if onlys* ...

But rather than subtracting, this final piece is about adding. A decade ago, I started adding each day of my life to my treasure of days lived. And with each day, my treasure started to grow, rather than diminish.

LIFE is the only game where the objective seems to be to work out the rules. And then, all too soon, just when you think you've figured out how to play the game, your time's up. Nobody truly knows where you go when you die but for the sake of this final section, please humour me and assume that we emigrate up there.

Let's call it 'The Cloud'.

In which case it's worth thinking about those who are already there. You might have loved ones who've passed away. Imagine them, sitting on The Cloud, looking down on us as we go about our day-to-day. Remember, these are the people who've had their time. They've lived their lives. They know all about *coulda, shoulda, woulda.* They've experienced their own personal *if onlys* ... .

And they love you, which means they're rooting for you.

Let's get silly and play around with what they're absolutely *not* saying. They're unlikely to be advising you to play small. Your heavenly cheerleaders aren't yelling for you to take no risks or shy away from opportunities or challenges. They're not urging you to spend more time scrolling on your phone or watching reality TV. They're not recommending that you carry a mediocre attitude around with you. They're not bellowing, 'Frown baby, frown.' They're not recommending that you slouch around and only come alive at weekends. They're not demanding that you should be full of self-doubt or cautious in love in case you get your heart broken.

The heavenly refugees have had their chance and they want you to make the most of yours!

They're up there, screaming at you to go for it! Seize every single day! Take some calculated risks and go for opportunities when they show up. I can hear them, screaming, 'If there aren't any opportunities, *create some!*' Get off your phone and look up, the world's amazing. Make eye contact with life. Smile. Be confident. Spend time with people you love. Quit procrastinating. Lose the excuses. Craft an attitude that makes people go wow. Get out of bed an hour earlier than everyone else and work on your secret long-term ambition. Eat the right foods, drink gallons of H_2O, get good quality sleep. It's okay to mess up. It doesn't matter if you sometimes fail or look silly. In fact, failure makes you stronger, and looking a bit silly is kind of sexy.

I 100% guarantee your heavenly champions are yelling for you to believe in yourself and squeeze the maximum value out of *every single moment of every single day*.

Those cloud dwellers are desperate for you to make the most of your time down there because, hey, one day it'll be your turn to emigrate to The Cloud.

So let's mess with your mind and visit *that* day. Your time is up!

It's foggy. You're barefoot, bewildered and you feel strangely light on your feet. There's a choir singing somewhere up ahead, so you put one foot in front of the other and walk towards the singing.

You waft away the thick mist and the wrought iron gates are picked out with a Vegas-style neon sign. The flashing arrow heralds your arrival: 'Welcome to the Afterlife'.

You join a long queue, shuffling forward as you watch a bearded gentleman sign people in. It's the same routine for everyone. He asks the person for their name and checks his list. Most, but not all, are nodded through.

Eventually, it's your turn. So let's imagine:

You're face-to-face with the impossibly old man, with eternal wrinkles. His name badge says, 'Saint Pete: Here to Help.'

It's a nerve shredding moment. You think the unthinkable. I mean, what if your name's *not* on the list?

It's not a time for banter. You give your full name and date of birth to the guardian of the eternal galaxy. Fingers and toes crossed …

Pete's old school. There's no tech, no spreadsheet, just a pregnant pause while the ancient man runs a bony finger down his list. His flicks to page two and you can't help yourself. The silence is deafening. You just have to speak.

'Does it work like Santa's nice list?' you joke. Then you're kicking yourself for saying it. Why am I even bothering to have banter with Saint Pete?

The old man looks up and raises a bushy eyebrow. He's seen and heard it all before. 'Nice is a low bar', he says. 'Up here, the boss is looking for a bit more. It's about impact', says the gatekeeper, matter-of-factly, his eyes turning back to the list, looking for your name. 'Have you made some sort of impression?' he mumbles. 'Was the world a better place for having you along for the ride? That kind of thing … Gotcha', he says.

And here's where my story ends.

Good news – *you're in*! Phew! You're not, you know, down there in that other place.

In the final reckoning, it's not about you versus the world, because the world would win every single time. It's not even you versus the other eight billion runners and riders in the human race.

The Guardian of the Eternal Galaxy isn't measuring you against anyone else. He's measuring you, against you. That's the only competition in town! If you can answer 'yes' (consistently) to the question *Am I a slightly better person than I was yesterday?* you'll be heading in the two-percenter direction.

Which means you can quit comparing. It's not about what anyone else is doing, it's about what YOU are doing.

'I don't want to get to the end of my life and find that I just lived the length of it. I want to have lived the width of it as well.'

Diane Ackerman. American poet.

Oh, and the ripple effect I've been banging on about since Chapter 1. Saint Pete's right. The clincher – your best self isn't just for you, it's for those you love the most.

To tie up all the loose ends here's a story that needs finishing, the show stealer from my wonderful co-author.

Previously, somewhere on the M1, just south of Sheffield …

Beads of sweat gathered on my brow. 'Can God do a handstand?' It's a sublime question from my four-year-old. I didn't want to venture into the ridiculous so I needed a great answer. This innocent drive was turning out to be quite a challenge.

My thoughts ran deep. *I'm not sure I even believe in God! If I did believe in him (her, it?), would him/her/it be able to do a handstand?*

In my mind's eye I could picture God as an old fella, up there somewhere, sitting in the clouds, or throwing bolts of lightning down at us. Sure he was wise. Omnipotent, even. But athletic? I'd never considered God to be athletic.

The motorway hummed by. I checked Olivia in the rear view mirror. She was waiting for my answer.

More thoughts flowed. *God's old, right? If my Sunday school teacher was correct, he's been around pretty much since the dawn of time. Maybe even longer. He probably invented time? And, again, if the religious texts are correct, he created Earth.*

My mind was wandering. *What preceded the Big Bang? Did God cause it?*

I missed my exit and came to my senses. *Chill, she's four.* I weighed up the evidence and came to the conclusion that God could probably do a forward roll, and possibly a star jump. *But a handstand, at his age?* My eyebrows met in the middle and I swerved to avoid a lorry.

After great deliberation I answered Olivia's question.

'Can God do a handstand? You know something sweetheart?' I said, glancing at my beautiful little girl in the rear view mirror. 'Probably not!'

I looked again. She seemed lost in thought. Had I given her the right answer?

A big smile appeared on her face as she replied in a very confident manner. 'Well Daddy, if he comes round to our house, I will show him how it's done.'

My eyebrows no longer met in the middle. They were raised in surprise. *'If he comes round to our house I'll show him how it's done!'* Was my little girl really willing to teach God how to do a handstand? How fantastic is that! And what a superb example of sharing best practice!

Or was my little girl challenging God to a head-to-head handstand competition round the back of a three-bed semi in Mansfield? My little girl against the omnipotent creator of life. If that's the case, whatever challenges we face seem feeble in comparison!

Summing it all up

Imagine you're 109 years old and, may I say, in very fine fettle. Must be all that oily fish! Imagine you're looking back on your life as it is TODAY. Then finish the following sentences:

I spent too much time worrying about . . .

_____

_____

_____

_____

_____

_____

I spent too little time doing things such as . . .

_____

_____

_____

_____

_____

_____

If I could go back in time, then what I would do differently from today onward is ...

_____

_____

_____

_____

_____

_____

_____

_____

_____

What are the two most important days of your life? Think hard. (The correct answer is at the bottom of the next page)

_____

_____

_____

_____

_____

_____

_____

That's all folks!

Our final note is a thank-you for reading *The Art of Being Brilliant*. If you've enjoyed it, please tell the world. A nice review would make our day.

> 'God heard us. He sent help. He sent you.'
>
> Marianne Williamson.
> American writer and politician

If you've hated it, well that's fine too. Apologies for putting you through it. We sincerely hope your day gets better.

Either way, even if you're not here to stay, we're eternally grateful that the universe allowed your soul to stop by.

In the words of Sgt Phil Esterhaus from 1980's cop show *Hill Street Blues*, 'Be careful out there', but I'd add, *not so careful that you miss out on all the fun!*

And *finally* finally, just in case nobody's told you yet today how absolutely, positively, incredibly amazing you are, we're telling you, right now.

You are truly radiant.

That will be all for today. Now pass it on.

Love:
Andy, Andy & Amy

#ArtOfBrillBook #BeMoreSeb #Lane10 #TheCloud #CanGodDoAHandstand

---

The two most important days of your life are, of course, today and tomorrow.

VENI
VIDI
AMAVI

WE CAME. WE SAW. WE L♥VED.

About the writing team

Dr Andy Cope is a keynote speaker, best-selling author, happiness expert and recovering academic. Andy has spent the past two decades researching the science of human flourishing, culminating in a Loughborough University PhD.

Andy's got enough self-awareness to understand that his 'Doctor of Happiness' moniker is terribly cheesy, but it does afford him an important media platform that he uses to help turn the narrative away from languishing, towards flourishing.

His findings are ploughed into his books and talks, and he now runs a training company that spreads the wellbeing messages far and wide. Art of Brilliance Ltd is set up on a not-for-profit basis, with all the surplus ploughed back into school and community projects. He's proud of the team's achievements, especially the Outstandingly Happy Schools programmes that have sprouted up all over the world.

Andy's literary career started out with the best-selling children's series 'Spy Dog' (Puffin Books) before branching out into happiness and wellbeing books for children, teenagers and adults.

He lives with his wife in Middle England. The have two grown up humans and the usual dog/cat story. They also have a bunch of hens and a couple of pet pigs, Hargreaves and Rooney, who, before you ask, are absolutely not for barbequing!

Email: andy@artofbrilliance.co.uk
Web: www.artofbrilliance.co.uk

Insta: TheHappyBloke   X: @beingbrilliant
Linked-In: art of brilliance   FB: art of brilliance

Andy Whittaker has been described as the best thing to come out of Morecambe since the M6 motorway. He's super-proud of his grown-up daughter, Olivia, who is making good things happen in her life.

At the time of writing the original version of this book Andy W and Andy C were mavericks of the training world, delivering high-quality but slightly edgy workshops and keynotes. Andy C played the clever PhD role, with Andy W specialising in rip-roaringly hilarious keynotes that would simultaneously change your life and cause you to wet yourself.

At that time, Andy Whittaker was probably the best keynote speaker on the planet. Andy C swears, hand on heart, that the top five keynotes he's ever seen have all been delivered by Andy W. Delegates would be literally crying with laughter.

At the peak of his success Andy W began to struggle with some deep-rooted personal problems and had to step back from the speaking circuit. It was a devastating blow, not just for Andy, but for conference delegates the world over. He was born to be a speaker. It's the only thing he's any good at!

For a while, there was a massive Andy Whittaker shaped hole on the speaking circuit. He's been working hard to fit the pieces of his life back together. Phoenix style, Andy Whittaker has a new website and is open for business.

Email: andy@theartofbeingbrilliant.com
Web: https://andywhittaker.uk/

Amy Bradley is a best-selling illustrator and designer, which basically means she draws pictures for a living. 'I know, pinch me!'

Fun, vibrant illustrations are right up her street but Amy's speciality is colour – it's her FAVE thing. It also just so happens she can pen many different styles of handwriting – you might have noticed a few in this book.

Amy's forever grateful that she gets to work with the amazing team at Art of Brilliance and says she owes much of her success to many themes in their books and workshops. By spooky coincidence, by bringing the books to life she's accidentally absorbed the ethos.

She's quick to point out that talent, effort and positivity are not the only drivers of her success. The fourth ingredient is CAKE! It's Victoria sponge that powers her towards tight publishing deadlines. Oh, and blueberry muffins.

Amy's currently training to run her first half marathon. There's not a day that goes by where you won't catch her going out for a power walk. She especially loves to visit and walk in the Lake District.

Amy's got a degree in art and illustration but she's well aware that there are many talented artists who end up working in coffee shops. She's spent over a decade drawing pictures for a living, and is super-proud and grateful to have been able to carve a career out of following her passion.

Email: amy@artofbrilliance.co.uk
Insta: amys_illos

Thanks for reading *The Art of Being BRILLIANT*. If you've enjoyed it, please tell the world and copy us in. If you've hated it, please keep quiet!

We figure that being your best self is actually quite easy but *staying* there is tricky. We don't want to leave you in limbo so we've created a whole host of ways to help you STAY BRILLIANT and that will keep you moving in the right direction.

Hey, here's the QR code. I'm pretty sure you've got it from here ...

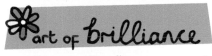

www.artofbrilliance.co.uk

FIND US | We're social

Clive's story

Clive wanted to be a superhero but despite consuming vast amounts of spinach, he remained puny. Clive had no sword of destiny or shield of truth. He couldn't jump tall buildings and although his specs cured his astigmatism, they didn't gift him X-ray vision.

Clive settled into his office job, his superhero career seemingly in tatters, when, one day, he went on a training course. To be clear, this wasn't any old training course, it was THE training course.

The one that rekindled his passion and ignited the fire in his belly.

It had a strange title. Silly even. While many of his work colleagues rolled their eyes at 'The Art of Being Brilliant', Clive remained open-minded. He was intrigued.

The first thing he noticed was that the trainer seems to care about their subject. And when I say care, I mean they *really* cared. It was plain speaking and simple, the exact opposite of death by PowerPoint. There were some funny bits but, somehow, Clive understood that the main message wasn't funny at all.

The curious thing about this workplace training is that it wasn't really about work.

'The Art of Being Brilliant' was about *life*.

And aliveness!
The trainer called it flourishing. It's an aliveness that leaks out of you and creates an uplift in others.

Clive was all in. He looked around and noticed that even the sceptics had shut their laptops! *Well, that's a first!*

Clive's ears pricked up when the trainer said that everyone in the room was a superhero, but that too many people were pretending to be normal.

And that was it! Bingo! *That's me!* thought Clive. *My superhero dream isn't extinct, it's just dormant.*

And, from that day forward, no ifs, no buts, Clive used the principles from 'The Art of Being Brilliant' to raise his game. At work, at home, with his mates, when visiting his mum ... Clive started to reveal his inner superhero.

Ironically, Clive lost the power of invisibility. But he gained *visibility* and self-respect. Plus a whole load of positivity, confidence, purpose, gratitude, creativity, kindness and resilience.

As Clive embraced these long-lost super-powers he began to shine.

That was four years ago and, guess what, Clive is still shining. He loves his work, his colleagues adore him and best of all, his customers can't get enough of him.

(Note to self, neither can his other half!)

Clive still can't jump tall buildings and try as he might, X-ray vision eludes him. Clive's found his super-power, which had been cunningly hidden as Clive! Clive 1.0 had been perfectly fine, but the upgrade to Clive 2.0 was lighting up the world.

Clive's currently considering taking it to the next level. *Is wearing my underpants on the outside a step too far?*

If you'd like the Clive experience, drop me an email to
andy@artofbrilliance.co.uk

ALSO BY ANDY COPE

Be Brilliant Every Day
Andy Cope & Andy Whittaker
9780857085009 · £10.99

The Little Book of Being Brilliant
Andy Cope
9780857087973 · £9.99

Shine: Rediscovering
Your Energy, Happiness
and Purpose
Andy Cope & Gavin Oattes
9780857087652 · £10.99

Zest: How to Squeeze
the Max out of Life
Andy Cope, Gavin Oattes
& Will Hussey
9780857088000 · £10.99

The Happiness Revolution:
A Manifesto for Living
Your Best Life
Andy Cope & Paul McGee
9780857088888 · £11.99

How to Be a Well Being:
Unofficial Rules to
Live Every Day
Andy Cope, Sanjeev Sandhu
& James Pouliopoulos
9780857088673 · £10.99

**Diary of a Brilliant Kid:
Top Secret Guide
to Awesomeness**
Andy Cope, Gavin Oattes
& Will Hussey
9780857087867 • £10.99

**Brill Kid -
The Big Number 2:
Awesomeness -
The Next Level**
Andy Cope, Gavin Oattes, Will
Hussey & Amy Bradley
9780857088918 • £10.99

**The Art of Being
A Brilliant Teenager,
2nd Edition**
Andy Cope & Amy Bradley
9780857089397 • £12.99

CAPSTONE
A Wiley Brand